C000217414

30 Days with Esther

Other books in the series:

30 Days with Mary:
A devotional journey with the mother of God

30 Days with Elijah:
A devotional journey with the prophet

30 Days with John:
A devotional journey with the disciple

30 Days with David:
A devotional journey with the shepherd boy

You can read more about Emily and her books
at:
www.emily-owen.com
facebook.com/EmilyOwenAuthor/
or
twitter.com/EmilyOwenAuthor

'Esther is brought into the twenty-first century as Emily crafts each daily devotional using this timeless story of royal intrigue and romance. Her use of this unique account about a young girl saving a nation, matched with life transforming Scripture, will enrich and inspire you. As we take this exciting journey with Esther, Emily shows how God is evident in each chapter and how he can make a difference in our lives.'

Veronica Alvarez, Regional Director (Europe),
Community Bible Study

'Emily Owen brings her Bible characters to life. Each day for 30 days you will get a snippet from their diary, and then be invited to reflect on your own life with the help of relevant Bible passages. The problem is the diary story is so good you will want to sneak a look at tomorrow, and the next day. Resist that temptation! Emily will give you plenty to chew on for one day at a time. Steadily the Bible character and the goodness of God will get under your skin and become part of you. So go on, get hooked on your daily dose . . .'

The Venerable Bob Jackson, former Archdeacon of Walsall,
conference speaker, author

30 Days with Esther

A devotional journey with the queen

Emily Owen

Authentic

Copyright © 2017 Emily Owen

23 22 21 20 19 18 17   7 6 5 4 3 2 1

First published 2017 by Authentic Media Limited,
PO Box 6326, Bletchley, Milton Keynes, MK1 9GG.
authenticmedia.co.uk

The right of Emily Owen to be identified as the Author of this Work
has been asserted by her in accordance with the
Copyright, Designs and Patents Act 1988.

All rights reserved.
No part of this publication may be reproduced, stored
in a retrieval system, or transmitted in any form or by any means,
electronic, mechanical, photocopying, recording or otherwise, without
the prior permission of the publisher or a licence permitting restricted
copying. In the UK such licences are issued by the Copyright Licensing
Agency, Barnard's Inn, 86 Fetter Lane, London EC4A 1EN.

British Library Cataloguing in Publication Data
A catalogue record for this book is available from the British Library.
ISBN: 978-1-78078-448-9
978-1-78078-450-2 (e-book)

Unless otherwise noted, all Scripture quotations taken from the Holy Bible,
New International Version Anglicised Copyright © 1979, 1984, 2011 Biblica.
Used by permission of Hodder & Stoughton Ltd, an Hachette UK company.
All rights reserved. 'NIV' is a registered trademark of Biblica UK trademark
number 1448790.

Scripture quotations noted isv are taken from the Holy Bible: International
Standard Version®. Copyright © 1996–forever by The ISV Foundation. ALL
RIGHTS RESERVED INTERNATIONALLY. Used by permission.

Scripture quotations noted GOD's WORD Translation are taken from GOD'S
WORD®, © 1995 God's Word to the Nations. Used by permission of Baker
Publishing Group.

Scripture quotations noted NLT are taken from the Holy Bible, New Living
Translation, copyright © 1996, 2004, 2007, 2013, 2015 by Tyndale House
Foundation. Used by permission of Tyndale House Publishers, Inc., Carol
Stream, Illinois 60188. All rights reserved.

Cover design by David McNeill revocreative.co.uk
Printed and bound by CPI Group (UK) Ltd, Croydon, CR0 4YY

for my granny (1927–2014)

Isaiah 30:21

Acknowledgements

I am fortunate to have many people 'be Esther' for me.
People who have come into my life at just the right time
and allowed God to use them 'for such a time as this'.
Thank you to each one.

Dave and Andrew.
Thank you for being there at just the right time
and pointing me in the right direction.

Esther asked people to pray for her
and, in this, I've 'been an Esther'.
Thank you to each person around the globe
who has responded to my requests for prayer.
You are valued more than I can say.

And thank you to God.
Always.

Introduction

A commoner who became Queen and saved her people.

Whose life changed and became something she'd never imagined.

Esther.

The story of Esther is gripping stuff.

Full of conspiracies, bravery, doubts, bravado, risks, celebrations, anger, humility.

As Esther goes through the ups and downs of life, her cousin, Mordecai, is never far away.

Encouraging her.

Challenging her.

Looking out for her.

The author of Esther is unknown, although some suggest Mordecai (cf. Esther 9:20).

Esther is the only book in the Bible in which God is not mentioned.

Explicitly, anyway.

He is implicit throughout.

Mordecai asks Esther:

'Who knows if perhaps you were made queen for just such a time as this?' (Esther 4:14, NLT)

Mordecai challenges Esther to live a godly life.

To ask, why?
Why am I here, right now?
And to believe that God knows exactly where she is.
In the bad times as well as the good.

Psalm 139:16 (NLT):

'You saw me before I was born.
Every day of my life was recorded in your book.
Every moment was laid out before a single day
had passed.'

Each day's reading ends with 'Esther's Quest' and is followed by 'My response'.

This is a challenge or thought for you to keep in mind as you go through your day, and write things down if you'd like to.

Esther 1:1:

'This is what happened during the time of Xerxes...'

Read *30 Days with Esther* to find out more.

It is my prayer that, as you read and reflect, you will draw closer to God.

The God who knows exactly where you are.

Right now.

'For such a time as this.'

Emily

Everything you say or do should be done in the name of the Lord Jesus, giving thanks to God the Father through him.

Colossians 3:17 (GOD'S WORD Translation)

Day 1

OK, so if I am going to keep a diary, I guess I'd better introduce myself.

My name is Esther and I live in the city of Susa in Babylon.

I live with Mordecai.

Mordecai used to live in Jerusalem but he was taken captive and brought to Susa.

We are Jews, that's why he was taken. And loads of other Jews were, too.

Mordecai is not my dad but he kind of is. He is actually my real dad's cousin. My mum and dad both died when I was small and that's when I went to live with Mordecai. He brought me up.

People say I am pretty but I don't really know about that. I just know that I like living with Mordecai and meeting my friends but I don't like the fact that some people in Babylon hate us Jews.

Can't think of anything else to say about myself really, so I will just have to hope that some interesting things happen, or I'm afraid this diary will be very boring . . .

Esther is an orphan living in a place that is not her natural home.
Somewhere with a different culture.
She could easily feel lost,
a bit of a misfit,
lacking in confidence,
someone who doesn't belong.

What about you?
As you go through life,
do you sometimes feel alone,
unsure,
confused,
a bit lost?

Let's look at a story Jesus told, Luke 15:

The story is about a sheep.
Who is living happily with the rest of the flock.
And all is well.
Then, one day, the sheep decides to go off on her own.
So away she goes,
trotting down lanes, past streams, over hills . . .
Further and further away.
She doesn't even look back once.
When she eventually stops, she has a look around.
And she does not recognize anything.

The trees are different.

The grass tastes different.

Even the sky looks different.

There are some other animals here and there, but none are like her.

The sheep wanders around a bit more,

trying to find something familiar,

something that will make her feel less lost.

But eventually she has to stop.

She's just going round in circles,

getting nowhere.

And she's exhausted.

So she lies down under an unfamiliar tree and goes to sleep.

Perhaps when she wakes up this will all be a bad dream.

But it isn't.

When she wakes up, nothing has changed.

The sheep looks around in despair.

The hours ahead seem endless and empty.

She prepares to face yet another day on her own.

And that's when she sees someone walking over a hill towards her.

The person gets closer and closer.

Could it really be?

The sheep thinks it might,

just might,

be her shepherd.

She hopes it is.

But she's not sure.
And then she finds herself being picked up.
And settled across a familiar pair of shoulders.
It is her shepherd, after all.
Come all this way.
Just to find her.
And suddenly, the sheep relaxes.
She stops worrying.

The trees are still different.
The grass still tastes different.
The sky still looks different.
The other animals still aren't like her.
But the sheep knows that everything will be OK.
Because she is with her shepherd.

Esther knew she'd be OK,
despite what was going on around her.
Because she was with Mordecai.
The sheep knew she'd be OK,
despite the environment around her.
Because she was with her shepherd.
What about you?
Whatever is going on in your life,
do you know
deep
down
that you'll be OK?
You'll be OK because God is right there with you.

Joshua 1:5:

'I will never leave you nor forsake you.'

Never.
Ever.
Ever.

Maybe, to the people around her in a strange city,
Esther was nothing special.
But she was special to Mordecai.
So much so that he adopted her.

Maybe you think you're nothing special.
Nothing special to other people.
Nothing special to yourself.

But you're special to God.

Ephesians 1:4,5:

*'In love he predestined us for adoption
to sonship through Jesus Christ, in accordance
with his pleasure and will.'*

God didn't make you a misfit.
In fact, the opposite is true.
He made you to fit.
Fit into the 'you-shaped gap' he made on purpose.
Because he wants you to fit right into his family.
As his beloved son or daughter.

As you begin this journey with Esther, make it your prayer that you will grow closer to the God – *Abba* – who loves you enough to adopt you into his family.

Father God,

Thank you that I am special to you.
I'm not a misfit.
I'm your child.
When life is hard, help me to remember that you're not going anywhere.
Help me to be as Esther was with Mordecai.
To feel safe simply because you're here with me.

Amen

Esther's Quest

God thinks
I'm special

My response:

Day 2

Well, so much for hoping that something interesting would happen; today has not been interesting at all. It was just the same old normal routine. In fact, if I write about it, I may send myself to sleep! I will give this diary-keeping thing one more go, I think, but if I still don't have anything to write about next time then I will just conclude that diaries and I don't really work very well together.

Do you ever feel like that?
That you're just going through the motions?
Going through the same old routine?

Let's look at Mark 12:

An elderly lady is walking slowly along.
She's on her way to the temple to give some money.

This is not an unusual journey for her.
She often goes to give.

No one notices her.
Everyone else is always too busy showing off how much money they are giving.

She doesn't show off.
Even if she wanted to there would be no point.
Because she doesn't have a lot of money to give.
She just quietly goes up,
gives her money,
and leaves.

But someone did notice her.
Someone did appreciate what she gave.
And that someone was Jesus.
He not only noticed her.
He used her as an example.
An example to teach his disciples about giving.

'She, out of her poverty, put in everything.'

The woman could have felt insignificant.
She was alone and poor.
Others around her were doing more.
They were giving more.
What was the point of putting in two small coins?
It was nothing compared with what everyone else gave.

They, out of their riches, put in something.

'She, out of her poverty, put in everything.'

The woman's 'everything' was small in comparison
with other people's 'something'.
But it had no limits.

Crucially, the 'something givers' are not condemned.
Giving is good.
Finance-giving, material-giving, time-giving.
But it's the wholehearted 'everything-giver' who is
commended.
By Jesus.

The woman was actually simply going through her
usual routine.
Doing what she often did.
Nothing new or exciting.
But:
Jesus noticed her.
Jesus watched her.
Jesus praised her.
For doing what she normally did.

Nothing new or different.

And it's the same for you.
When you are doing the school run,
or holding a coffee morning,
or gardening,
or going to work or school,
or doing the shopping,
or DIY,
or cleaning the house,
or washing the car;
normal, mundane things . . .

Jesus notices you.

Never think that what you do is not appreciated.

The woman gave glory to God by simply living her life. Her story has been told again and again.

Do you give glory to God by simply living your life?

By living the life he's given you?

Colossians 3:17 (NLT):
'Whatever you do or say, do it as a representative of the Lord Jesus, giving thanks through him to God the Father.'

You are a representative of the Lord Jesus!

Whatever you do, however mundane,
will you represent him well today?

You can be sure that he'll notice . . .

Father God,

You know the things that will come my way today.
I don't.
Whatever happens today, I ask you to help me.
Help me to be your representative.
To be wholehearted.
To be an everything-giver.
To show by the way I live that I belong to you.

Amen

Esther's Quest

Be an
everything-giver

My response:

Day 3

Maybe diaries and I do work well together after all. I have something big to write about today! Everyone is talking about what happened at the palace last night.

For the past week, King Xerxes has been throwing one big party. At the same time, Queen Vashti has been throwing one for the women. Last night the King called for the Queen to come and join his party. He sent a message telling her to put on her crown and come to him so that he could show off her beauty to his guests (Queen Vashti is one of the most beautiful people I have ever seen).

Xerxes calls for Vashti.
He wants to show her off.
He's proud of her.

What about you?
Do you make God proud?
By how you live,
what you think,
what you say?

Xerxes wanted to show his guests a queen.
A living example of what a queen should be.
And he chose Vashti.

If God wanted to show an example of someone living
a godly life,
would he choose you?
Would he be able to choose you?

Look at what God said about David, Acts 13:22:
'I have found David son of Jesse, a man after my own
heart; he will do everything I want him to do.'

Could you swap David's name for yours?
Can God confidently say about you:
Here's someone who will do everything I want
them to?
Who will live my way?
Who will make me proud?

And can you confidently say it about yourself?
I'm someone who lives God's way?

Paul, in his letter to the church in Philippi, after telling
them how to live as followers of Jesus, gives them one
final tip (4:9a):
'Whatever you have learned or received or heard from
me, or seen in me – put it into practice.'

Paul was so close to God,
he could be confident that,
whatever God wanted him to do,
he would do it.
And his life bears testimony to the truth of this.
Paul lived a life that said:
I will do whatever God wants me to.
Full stop.

Do you?
Or do you swap the full stop for 'except'?
'I'll do anything . . . except give up my time/
possessions/popularity/etc.'?

Let's look at Mark 10:

A man is walking.
His feet are dragging.
His face is downcast.
In the background is Jesus.
Ahead of the man is his lavish home.
Jesus gets smaller and the house gets bigger.

A few minutes before, the man and Jesus had been
having a conversation, which went something like
this:

Man: What do I need to do to be sure of having eternal life?
It has been said that eternity starts now.

So the man is basically saying, how can I be truly alive from now on?

Jesus: You know what the commandments are – don't kill, don't steal, don't lie . . .

Man: Oh, that's OK then. I've kept all of those commandments ever since I was a child. So I guess I have eternal life after all. Phew.

Jesus: Well, there is one more thing. Sell everything you have, give it to the poor and then follow me.

And that's why the man is walking in the wrong direction.
Away from Jesus.
That's why the man is sad.
His wealth was his 'except'.
And his 'except' was stopping him from really following Jesus.

What about you?
What are your 'excepts'?
The things you cling on to, not willing to release them to God?
The things that put him in the background?

The things that stop you being truly alive?

John 10:10:
'[Jesus said]: "I have come that they may have life, and have it to the full."'

Xerxes doesn't only ask Vashti to come, he asks her to wear her crown.

The crown would show everyone that she was the Queen.

Show them that she was Xerxes' wife.

When we receive the abundant life that Jesus offers, he gives us a crown.

A crown that says, this person belongs to me.

A crown that says, I've got it covered.

A crown that says, I'm pleased with this person.

A crown that says, this person brings me joy.

A crown that says, this person can truly live.

Isaiah 62:2–4 (NLT):

*'And you will be given a new name
by the LORD's own mouth.
The LORD will hold you in his hand for all to see –
a splendid crown in the hand of God.
Never again will you be called "The Forsaken City"
or "The Desolate Land."
Your new name will be "The City of God's Delight"
and "The Bride of God,"
for the LORD delights in you
and will claim you as his bride.'*

Day 3

Father God,

Sometimes I am like the rich man.
There are things I want to keep for myself.
And so I shove you into the background.
I walk away, heading in the wrong direction.
And I am sad inside.
Help me to be someone that you and I can both
have confidence in.
Confidence that I'll keep facing the right way.
Facing true life.
And confidence that I won't let anything get in the
way of finding your heart.
Or of wearing your crown.

Amen

Esther's Quest

Don't leave God in
the background

My response:

Day 4

But Vashti didn't want to join Xerxes' party, so she said no. She actually said no to the King! When Vashti said no to him, Xerxes got really angry. I think he was embarrassed that she'd made him look stupid in front of his guests. Well, in front of the whole city really, I guess, since this is the only thing people are talking about.

The King called a meeting with his advisors and asked them what the law said he should do. They said that Vashti had openly disobeyed the King and that this must be dealt with. Otherwise all the wives in the kingdom would follow her example and think that it was OK for them to disrespect their husbands, too. They advised the King to refuse to let Vashti into his presence ever again, and to look for a new queen instead. Which is what the King did.

Now he is searching all of Susa on the lookout for a new queen. Imagine being chosen to be the bride of the King! I wonder what she'll be like?

Examples can be a powerful thing, can't they?
Sometimes actions really do speak louder than words.
As Christians, the way we live and the example we set
are so important.
The world is watching.

Titus 2:7:
'In everything set . . . an example by doing what is good.'

'In everything.'
Every.
Thing.

What sort of 'in everything' example does your life set
for those around you?

Let's look at Moses:
Moses was called by God to do something.
That something was to lead the nation of Israel, over
two and a half million people,[1] into the land that God
had promised them.
He was called to get all these people from A to B.
He was called to be their leader.
He was called to be the link between the people and
God.
And Moses was scared.
He didn't think he'd be up to the job.
He wasn't confident.
He spoke hesitantly.

He stuttered.
He tried to persuade God to find someone else.
Someone who'd make a better go of things.

Fast forward:
Moses has been doing the job for a while.
Yes, there have been difficulties along the way.
But, overall, he's led the people well.

One day, however, Moses will die.
And so a new leader needs to be found.

Joshua is introduced as Moses' assistant.
He goes up the mountain with Moses to receive
the Ten Commandments, and sees a cloud envelop
Moses as he enters God's presence (Exodus 24).
Joshua was one of the twelve men chosen to go and
spy out the promised land when the Israelites got
close enough to be able to take a look (Numbers 13:8).
Joshua hears the wonderful final words of Moses
as Moses blesses each of the tribes by name
(Deuteronomy 33).

So, just from these three examples, Joshua has seen
Moses to be
a man who is close to God,
a man who knows his people well enough to be able
to delegate,
and a man who passes on God's blessings to them.

What an example Moses left for Joshua to follow:
Spiritually: He was close to God.
Intellectually: He thought about other people.
Emotionally: He invested in other people. He cared about them.

What sort of example do you leave for others?

Maybe you think not a very good one . . .

Remember, Moses could only be the example he was because he had allowed God to use him.
To mould him.
To change him.
To refine him from a man who said,
'I can't do that, no matter what God says,'
to a man who said,
'I can do that, because God says.'

The world is watching.

Paul concluded his letter to the church in Philippi with these words:

Philippians 4:9:
'Whatever you have learned or received or heard from me, or seen in me – put it into practice. And the God of peace will be with you.'

Basically, if you want to know how to live a godly life,
copy me.
Follow my example.

If someone imitated you and the way you live,
would they be living a godly life as a result?

Moses wasn't always the example-setter he became.
But, with God's help, he overcame his fears.
He overcame his weaknesses.
His lack of self-confidence.
And he became the first leader of God's people.
Moses overcame.
He dealt with stuff.

Xerxes did, too.
He had a situation on his hands:
Vashti, his Queen, had openly defied him.
The example Xerxes set by the way in which he dealt
with that situation would affect the whole of his
kingdom.
So he dealt with it quickly.
He identified the problem,
the probable repercussions
and he dealt with them.

It's a good example to follow.
When faced with a difficult situation, try to deal with
it rather than bury it and hope it will go away.

And how do we deal with our difficult situations?
Well, we hand them to God.
Sounds easy, doesn't it?
But maybe we're not always very good at what comes next:
Living in the light of that handover.

Psalm 55:22:

'Cast your cares on the LORD and he will sustain you.'

Sustain.
Support.
Care for.
Enable to keep going.
Draw alongside.
Encourage.
Nourish.

Living in the light of handing over your problems to God means being sustained.
Sustained by God.
And when you live sustained by God, you are an overcomer.
By definition.
You can deal with stuff.
By definition.

Day 4

Father God,

I'm not sure how I feel about being an example.
People should learn how to follow you by watching
and learning from me?
That challenges me.
I feel like saying with Moses:
please choose someone else.
But I know that's a cop out.
Help me to step up to the plate and be able to say
with Paul, imitate me.
For your glory, Lord.
In everything.

Amen

Esther's Quest

Hand over to God

My response:

Day 5

A lot can happen in a year! My quiet, normal life with Mordecai seems like another world. For the past twelve months, I have been living in the King's palace! Maybe people who said I was pretty were not wrong after all – King Xerxes ordered that the most beautiful girls in his kingdom be brought to live in the palace, and I was one of them!

I have not actually seen the King yet, I had to have a year of beauty treatments first, but I am going to see him tomorrow. I am so nervous. Plus the fact I have been told I can take anything I want to the King's palace with me. Great. I've no idea what to take; think I will just ask the man in charge of us for some advice on that one. I am shaking in my shoes about tomorrow. What if the King doesn't like me? If he's not pleased with me, if he doesn't call my name, that's it – I won't be allowed back here. I am scared.

I don't know what is going on in my life right now. Mordecai is still being brilliant; every day he comes down to the courtyard to see how I am getting on. But it's not the same as having him and my friends to talk to. I am glad I have my diary . . .

Esther has been chosen.
Chosen to go before the King.
But not before a time of preparation.
A time of cleansing.

Did you know that you've also been chosen?
Chosen by God to stand in his presence without spot
or blemish.
And you can only do that because Jesus prepared
the way.
Because he made you clean.

Colossians 1:22:
*'He has reconciled you by Christ's physical body through
death to present you holy in his sight, without blemish
and free from accusation.'*

Holy.
Set apart as special.
Without blemish.
All the bad stuff gone.
Free from accusation.
Confidently holding your head high.

So, for a whole year, Esther has been anticipating her
appearance before the King.
Waiting for the moment when she will actually see
him.
With her own eyes.

Day 5

Let's look at Zacchaeus, Luke 19:

Zacchaeus has heard about Jesus.
In fact, he's heard a lot about Jesus.
But he has never really seen him.
He's wanted to, though.
Maybe even tried to.
The thing is; Zacchaeus is very small.
He can never see over the heads of the crowd
surrounding Jesus.
But none of that matters now.

Because today Zacchaeus is definitely going to see
Jesus.

He knows he will.
He has laid his plans carefully.
After checking the route that Jesus will be taking,
rather than wait and hope he'll be able to see,
Zacchaeus has climbed a tree.
He is sitting in that tree right now.
Any moment, Jesus will come walking along the road.
And Zacchaeus will see him.
Because he's looking out.

What about you?
Have you seen Jesus?
If not, maybe you keep trying but don't seem to quite
get there?

Well, are you really looking out for him?
Really?
And if so, have you got yourself into the best place to
see him?

Standing beside the road was probably an obvious
place to wait and see Jesus.
It worked for lots of people.
But it didn't work for Zacchaeus.
So Zacchaeus had to do something different.

Maybe, as you look around,
it seems that other people are
close to God,
worshipping God,
getting to know God,
coming to God in very similar ways to each other.
But those ways are just not working for you.
You can't quite see over the crowd
to Jesus.

Well, be like Zacchaeus.
Remember that seeing Jesus is much more important
than the route you take to see him.
Be different if you need to be.
God is a God of individuals.
And he's OK with different.

So, Zacchaeus climbed the tree.
He parted the branches.
His eyes strained towards the horizon,
in the direction that he knew Jesus would be coming
from.
And finally, after all that waiting, he saw him.
Zacchaeus saw Jesus.
With his own eyes.
No one else's.
His very own.

Don't give up.
Jesus will be there.

1 Corinthians 2:9 (NLT):
*'No eye has seen, no ear has heard,
and no mind has imagined what God
has prepared for those who love him.'*

For Zacchaeus, what God had prepared for him was
to welcome Jesus into his home for a meal.
But, if Zacchaeus had been unwilling to put Jesus
before convention,
he'd never have known the joy
of welcoming Jesus as a guest.

What has God got in store for you?

Don't let tradition hold you back from the God who made you an individual.
And who wants you to come to him as an individual.

Don't miss out on joy.

Psalm 139:1:
'LORD . . . you know me.'

Father God,

Help me to keep looking out for you.
And to do whatever it takes to see you.
You're a God of individuals.
I'm an individual.
So you're my God.
Thank you that you know me.
That you made me.
That you want to spend time with me.
Thank you that, with you, different is OK.

Amen

Esther's Quest

God made me me

My response:

Day 6

I was walking in the courtyard today and people bowed before me and called me 'Queen Esther'. Yes, that's right; out of all the girls, the King chose me!

When I became his Queen, Xerxes gave a big banquet for all his nobles and officials. He said it was my banquet, so I guess they all came because of me – wow.

I look different now but I am still the same girl inside, so I am obeying Mordecai. He told me to keep the fact that I am a Jew to myself, which is what I've done. No one in the palace knows my background.

It's party time!
Esther has become Queen.
So Xerxes throws a party.

Have you ever had a party thrown for you?
Maybe your birthday, or wedding, or graduation?
Or maybe you haven't.
Maybe you feel as though no one really celebrates you.

Day 6

Let's look at Luke 15:

A man is throwing a big party.
He's invited all his friends and neighbours.
They are celebrating in style . . .
But why?
Well, earlier that day, the man had gone to count his sheep.
He knew he had 100 sheep.
So why could he only count ninety-nine?
He counted again.
Ninety-nine.
And again.
Ninety-nine.
At last, he realized why.
He'd not miscounted:
One sheep was missing.
'Oh, it's only one,' the man could have thought.
'I've still got ninety-nine,' he could have thought.
'It'll probably come back on its own,' he could have thought.
But he didn't think any of these things.
Instead, he locked the ninety-nine sheep away safely.
And set off.
Over hills.
Through streams.
Climbing rocks.
Constantly on the lookout for his sheep.

At last, he finds her.
He picks her up.
He carries her home.
And he throws a big party.
The sheep is no longer lost.
And that's worth celebrating.

Luke 15:7 (NLT):
'There is more joy in heaven over one lost sinner who repents and returns to God than over ninety-nine others who are righteous and haven't strayed away!'

Are you lost?
You don't need to be, you know.

Jesus said, 'I am the good shepherd' (John 10:14).

Stop running and let the Shepherd find you.
Then you'll be no longer lost.
And heaven will have a great big party,
just for you.

So, exciting times for Esther:
She's become Queen.
She's having parties thrown for her.
She has people waiting on her.
And yet, she's still Esther.
Essentially the same.
Still the girl who obeys her uncle.

Esther doesn't let what's happening to her go to
her head.

What about you?
It can be easy to want to take the glory for things that
we do or that happen to us, can't it?
Or even if we don't actively want to take the glory, we
forget to give God the glory.
Which amounts to the same thing.

Daniel (in the book of Daniel) had every opportunity
to take the glory for himself.
He was strong.
Handsome.
Intelligent.
And he'd interpreted a dream for the King.
A dream that no one else could interpret.
He's done pretty well.
Every opportunity to take the glory for himself.
And yet he doesn't.
'I can't do any of this.
But God can.'

Give God the glory.
Because God's the one that can.

It's easy to remember that we can't do things in our
own strength when we find them difficult, isn't it?
Or when we find them tiring.

Or when we can't be bothered.
Or we don't want to do them anyway.
Not really.

At times like these, praying for God's strength comes fairly easily.

But what about when we find things easy?
When the thing we are doing or being asked to do comes very naturally to us?
Well, God doesn't go away and leave us to it.
He is still there.
Enabling us.
Guiding us.
Strengthening us.
Or at least he wants to be.

But sometimes we don't let him.
We can manage on our own.
And maybe we do manage on our own.
But isn't it better to bring God on board and more than manage?

Philippians 4:13 (ISV):
'I can do all things through him who strengthens me.'

All things.
And that includes the hard things, the easy things, the boring things, the exciting things, the tricky things . . .

Everything you do,
do it in God's strength.
For his glory.

Father God,

Thank you that you chose me.
There are billions of people in the world.
And yet you still chose me.
Chose me to belong to you.
Chose me to receive your strength.
Chose me to give you glory.
I'm sorry for the times I do things in my own strength.
From now on, I want my whole life to be lived in your strength.
And lived for your glory.

Amen

Esther's Quest

God can

My response:

Day 7

The King nearly got killed today! I am so thankful for Mordecai: If it wasn't for him, my husband would be dead right now.

Mordecai overheard two of the King's officials having a bit of a debate. Things got heated and they both got really angry. They were angry at Xerxes I think, 'cos they started forming a plan to assassinate him. I have no doubt that they'd have gone through with it, too. But Mordecai told me and I told the King, who had the officials killed instead.

Of course, I made sure Xerxes knew that it was Mordecai who had saved his life, and Xerxes had it written down in the official records.

Good old Mordecai strikes again.
He's in the right place at the right time.

Where was the right place for Mordecai?
It was by the King's Gate.
Mordecai was sitting.
By the gate.
Of the palace.
He was not inside, enjoying the luxury of royal life.

He was sitting
by the
gate.
And yet he was exactly where he was meant to be.

Maybe, as you look around you,
you seem to be stuck by the gate.
Watching the hustle and bustle of life as it happens.
But from a bit of a distance.
Not able to fully join in.
You're surrounded by people who seem to have it
easy.
And life is not easy for you.
It's a struggle.
It's mundane.
It's hard.

Let's look at John 21:

Two men are walking along a beach.
They are deep in conversation.
One is Peter.
The other is Jesus.
Jesus has just been giving Peter a job to do.

Imagine, being given a special job by Jesus!

Peter could hardly believe that he,
after all his failings,
still had a place in Jesus' plan.

Wow.

But then Peter turns round.

Maybe he's distracted.

Maybe he wants to see what else is out there.

Whatever, he is clearly not completely focused on Jesus and what Jesus is asking him to do.

So he turns round.

And that's when he sees John.

Which makes him wonder . . .

Which leads to Peter pointing to John and asking Jesus,

'What about him?'

What about him?

You've just told me that although I've got a special job to do, my life won't be easy and I'll die a painful death.

What about him, though?

Is he going to get a better deal than me?

And what does Jesus say?

'Don't worry about him.

You just need to follow me.'

In other words:

You just need to do what I am asking you to do.

And what I am not asking you to do is to be so concerned about what's happening around you that it stops you from focusing on me.

Stops you hearing me.

Stops you following me.

'Don't worry about him.

Don't compare yourself with him.

You just need to follow me.'

John would have his own job to do.
Just as Mordecai did.
Just as Esther did.
Esther couldn't have overheard the plot by the gate.
But Mordecai couldn't have spoken to the King
about it.
They each had to focus on and fulfil their individual
roles.
Which, for Mordecai, meant sitting by a gate.
Maybe not exciting but definitely essential.

1 Peter 4:10 (NLT):
*'God has given each of you a gift from his great variety
of spiritual gifts. Use them well to serve one another.'*

Peter wrote these words.
Peter, who was once so concerned
about what others were doing.
He could say, each of you has your own gift.
Your own job to do.
Use it well.

The King was able to stop the assassination plot
because Esther told him about it.
Esther told him about it because Mordecai had
told her.
Mordecai told Esther about it because he had
overheard it being discussed.
And Mordecai overheard it being discussed because ...
he sat by the gate.

Maybe God is asking you to sit by the gate?
To serve him in the midst of the normal ups and
downs of life.
And to focus on him.
Rather than look around and say, 'What about them . . .?'

And don't think what you do goes unnoticed.
Just as Xerxes recognized Mordecai's faithfulness by
having his name in the book of official records, so
God will recognize everything you do.

1 Samuel 2:30:
'Those who honour me, I will honour.'

Father God,

Help me not to look around all the time,
Comparing myself with others.
Help me to focus on you as I go through my week.
Through my day.
Through my minutes.
I want to sit by the gate, ready to do whatever you
want me to do.
Lord, it's a privilege to serve you.
A privilege that's mine.
And the fact that you honour me in it is
mind-blowing.
Thank you.

Amen

Esther's Quest

Focus on God

My response:

Day 8

Mordecai is in trouble. In fact, he has got all the Jews in trouble. I love Mordecai and I really admire the way he sticks to his principles and convictions, but sometimes I wonder if he should just bow down. Xerxes has promoted a man named Haman; Haman is now the highest ranking of all the nobles. The King told everyone that they must bow down in respect whenever Haman passed through the King's Gate.

As soon as I heard about this, I just knew that Mordecai would refuse. And I was right. So he was reported to Haman. Haman was told not only that Mordecai wouldn't bow down, but also that Mordecai is a Jew.

The former made Haman furious and the latter gave him a plan: Rather than just kill Mordecai, Haman is now looking to destroy all the Jews in the land! And I am a Jew, but I've still not told anyone . . .

Principles.
We all have them.
Principle: A rule that forms the basis for a system of behaviour.
And we try to stick with them.
Whether or not we manage may have something to do with how important a principle is to us.

Mordecai had a principle.
And that principle was not to bow down to Haman.
So he didn't.
But that doesn't mean it was easy.

Let's look at Jesus, Matthew 4:

Jesus had just been baptized when the devil decided to follow him into the desert.
And tempt him to do things he shouldn't.
At the baptism, God's voice had rung out,
'This is my Son, whom I love' (Matthew 3:17).
When temptations come,
remind yourself that God loves you.
Jesus had just heard God.
He'd heard God loud and clear.
I love you.
Jesus wasn't facing temptations alone,
he was facing them surrounded by God's love.

What about you?
When you face tough times?

When you try desperately not to want to do something you desperately want to do but know you shouldn't?
Take a minute to stop and remind yourself that you are protected.
Protected by a God who loves you very much.
You're surrounded by him.

Psalm 139:5 (isv):

'You encircle me from back to front, placing your hand upon me.'

Encircled.
Every way you turn, God is.
His love.
His enabling.
His protection.

So, just what were these temptations Jesus faced?
The first one was to turn stones into bread.
Because he was hungry.
The second was to jump off the highest point of the temple.
To prove that God could save him.
The third was to bow down and worship the devil.
In return for all the kingdoms of the world.
The devil tempted Jesus physically, emotionally and spiritually.
And each time, Jesus responded by quoting the Bible.

The Bible is a wonderful defence mechanism:
It's worth getting to know.

Jesus had been fasting for forty days.
He'd have been hungry.
More than hungry.
The Bible quote he chose?
'Man does not live on bread alone but on every
word that comes from the mouth of the LORD'
(Deuteronomy 8:3).

We need spiritual nourishment.

1 Peter 2:2,3:
*'Like newborn babies, crave pure spiritual milk, so that
by it you may grow up in your salvation, now that you
have tasted that the Lord is good.'*

Powerfully desire (crave) spiritual nourishment:
Want it.
Seek it.
Chase it.
It's the best food you can have.

Think back to the last time you were hungry.
What did you do?
Well, you probably had something to eat.
And, as far as possible, you probably eat regularly so
that you never get too hungry.
What about spiritually?

Day 8

Do you feed yourself enough?
Spending time with God and his word?

People who want to lose weight often start eating
less and so, over time, their stomach shrinks.
They stop having the capacity to eat much.
How's your spiritual stomach?
Is it shrinking through lack of nourishment?
Is its capacity reduced to a nibble here and there?
If so, is that what you want?
Do you want to be on a 'lose spiritual weight fast' diet?
Or would you prefer to be on a 'banquet every day' diet?
Because the banquet is there for the taking.
The bigger the better.
Don't stop growing spiritually.
Our God is infinite.
No matter how much you grow, you'll never need
to stop.

And, the more you know of God, the more you'll want
to know of God.

So, Haman wanted to punish Mordecai for his
principles.
But also for who he was.
For being a Jew.

Mordecai had the option to deny his principles if he
wanted to.

He had no choice about his nationality, though.
He was a Jew, through and through.
There was no hiding it.

What about you?
Are you a follower of Jesus, through and through?
In a way that's obvious?
Or are you a follower of Jesus in a sometimes-hidden way?
In a 'blink and you'll miss it' way?
In a 'when it suits me' way?

1 Peter 2:12 (NLT):
'Be careful to live properly among your unbelieving neighbors. Then even if they accuse you of doing wrong, they will see your honorable behavior, and they will give honor to God when he judges the world.'

'Live properly' in the world.
And before God.

But Haman didn't only want to punish Mordecai
He wanted to punish all the Jews in the land because of Mordecai.
Haman wanted to punish all because of one.
Because he was angry with one.

Let's turn that the other way:
There was a time when one was punished because of all.

Day 8

Punished although he was the only one who has
never done anything wrong.
Jesus.
Punished for all who have done wrong.
Again and again.
Everyone.
Jesus was punished for me.
Jesus was punished for you.
'The Lord laid on him the sins of us all' (Isaiah 53:6b, NLT).

Jesus was whipped.
Thorns were twisted into a crown and rammed on his
head.
His hands were nailed to a cross.
He was stabbed in the side.
Pain.
Pain.
Pain.
And yet the biggest pain of all,
the thing that hurt most,
was when darkness came.
Sin came.
'The Lord laid on him the sins of us all' (Isaiah 53:6b, NLT).

Alone in the darkness,
Jesus cried in agony to God: 'Why have you forsaken
me?' (Matthew 27:46).
Pain.
Pain you'll never need to know.

Words you'll never need to say.
Darkness you'll never need to know.
Because Jesus knew it for you.
There, in the darkest of dark,
Jesus took the punishment for every sin that has ever
been committed.
Including yours.
Anything that you have ever done wrong was dealt
with at the cross.

Which is why, every time you give in to temptation
or lose your way
or neglect your spiritual nourishment
or hide the fact that you follow God,
all you need to do is turn to him and say
sorry.
And hear him reply:

'My child, it's OK.
It really is.
This has been dealt with.
So let go.
Come here.
And we'll move on.
You and I.
Together.'

Psalm 103:12:
'As far as the east is from the west, so far has he removed our transgressions from us.'

Believe it.

Because it's true . . .

Father God,

As I live my life, help me to have principles that reflect your own.
And help me have the courage to stick with them.
Let the way I live make it impossible for me to deny that I follow you.
Thank you that you've dealt with the times I mess up.
Thank you that you want to move on, together.
I love saying 'together' about you and me!
Thank you for making it possible.

Amen

Esther's Quest

Don't go on a
spiritual diet

My response:

Day 9

I don't believe it: Haman has actually persuaded the King to go along with destroying the Jews. Haman said that the Jews don't obey the King's laws and that they have customs that are different from everyone else, so it was in the King's best interests to destroy them before things got out of hand. And the King actually agreed!

Letters have been sent to all the governors, telling them to destroy every Jew who lives in their area and even telling them the day on which to do it. If they don't do it, they will be breaking the law. And the letters have been sent in lots of different languages, so that everyone will understand what's going on.

My people understand only too well and are terrified. I understand too, but there is nothing I can do. Haman and Xerxes are determined and are even celebrating their plan over a drink.

Apparently, Haman is afraid.

Afraid of the Jews and the fact that they stick to their beliefs and customs.

But hang on a minute.

Haman has just had a brilliant career move.

He's been promoted.

He is now the highest ranking of all the nobles in the land.

Second only to the King.

Surely he should be feeling confident.

And yet Haman seems to be afraid.

Afraid of the Jews.

Haman, the man promoted and esteemed by the King, is feeling threatened by the Jews.

Threatened by what they could do to the kingdom and, therefore, what they could do to his position within the kingdom.

It's as though Haman is not totally secure in who the King has made him to be.

What about you?

How secure are you in who God has made you to be?

Actually, who has he made you to be?

Do you know?

You have been made to be:

Valued.

Worthy.

Loved.

Precious.

In Isaiah 43:4 (NLT) God says: 'You are precious to me.
You are honored, and I love you.'

Do you know that?
Really know?
And do you believe it?

Try saying: 'I am precious and honoured and loved by
God.'

But what about the times when, like Haman, you
begin to worry?
You begin to doubt your position?
Maybe because you don't think you're worth it,
or you mess up,
or you're not very nice:

John 10:28:
'No one will snatch them out of my hand.'

No one.
Or anything.

Nothing can snatch you out of God's hand.

You're angry.
Nothing can snatch you out of his hand.
You're jealous.
Nothing can snatch you out of his hand.

You're confused.
Nothing can snatch you out of his hand.
You're dejected.
Nothing can snatch you out of his hand.
You're overwhelmed.
Nothing can snatch you out of his hand.
You're full of regrets.
Nothing can snatch you out of his hand.
You're exhausted.
Nothing can snatch you out of his hand.
You're . . .
Nothing can snatch you out of his hand.

Nothing at all.
Because he doesn't want anything to.
So he made sure nothing could.

Isaiah 49:16:
'See, I have engraved you on the palms of my hands.'

Engraved.
Etched on.
Permanent.

Perhaps Haman felt that he had to do things (persecute the Jews) in order to be able to keep his position.
He needed to work it all out himself.
But his position was secure.
After all, the King himself gave it to him.
All he needed to do was just be.

Day 9

Perhaps you feel you have to do things in order to keep your position with God.
But your position is secure.
Engraved on the palms of his hands.
You can just be.

For Mordecai, sticking to his beliefs and principles had a direct effect on others.
Namely, on the Jews.
His refusal to bow to Haman was going to make things very difficult for them.
But, for Mordecai, bowing down would have been wrong.
And nothing came between him and doing the right thing.

What about you?
As you look at yourself, are you sometimes stopped from doing the right thing simply because of the direct effect that it may have on other parts of your life?
For example, don't give money to something because you'll be left without means to treat yourself.
Or don't stop and talk to someone: You know they need a listening ear but you also know that it will take a lot of time which, quite frankly, you don't want to give.

Let's look again at the rich young ruler, Mark 10:

Jesus has just told a young man exactly how he can
follow Jesus.
How he can have a closer relationship with him.
But the man is sad.
He thought he was OK,
but then Jesus asked for his money.
'Anything but that,' thought the man.
'That's just more than I can give.'
He probably thought of his house.
Of parties he threw for his friends.
Of the status his money allowed him to enjoy.
There was no way he could give up those things.

What he possibly didn't think was:
Is this more than I can give?
Or is this more than I am willing to give?

God won't ask us to do more than we can.
And, when we think we can't but he knows we can, he
gently whispers:
You can do this.
You can.
And here's how:

2 Corinthians 12:9 (NLT):
*'My grace is all you need. My power works best in
weakness.'*

So, if Jesus doesn't ask for more than we can give, it is pretty safe to assume that the honest answer to that question is that money was more than the man was *willing* to give.

Honesty is so important in relationships.
Relationship with others.
Relationship with ourselves.
And relationship with God.
It's impossible to hide anything from him,
so why do we even try?
Actually, why do we even want to?

Psalm 38:9 (NLT):
'You know what I long for, Lord; you hear my every sigh.'

There is security in being known by a loving God.

When Xerxes issued his decree, he did so in many different languages.
He wanted to be sure that everyone understood.
The message was the same but not everyone could receive it in exactly the same way.

We have a God who treats us as individuals,
who loves us as individuals,
who speaks to us as individuals.

And, because we are all different, it follows that we'll be treated differently.
Treated differently by a God who loves us equally.

I am precious and honoured and loved by God.

Father God,

Thank you that you're not me.
I'd have given up on me long ago.
But you never do.
You're always there, drawing me back to you.
Strengthening me.
Comforting me.
Encouraging me.
Saying, 'We'll do this together.'
Help me to remember that we're always together.
Lord, sometimes I compare our relationship/myself with other people.
Help me know that different doesn't mean differently loved,
and to be secure in your love for me.

Amen

Esther's Quest

I'm individually
but equally loved

My response:

Day 10

Or maybe there is something I can do to help.
Mordecai thinks there is, anyway. But it's all right
for him, he's not the one who's actually got to do it.

Here's what happened today: Mordecai found out
what had been ordered for all the Jews, and he was
devastated. He wept loudly, put on sackcloth and
ashes and sat at the King's Gate. My maids came
and told me and of course I was really upset that
Mordecai was in this state. It upset me to think
of him in sackcloth, so I sent him some clothes to
put on instead, but he refused them. Then I sent
someone else to talk to Mordecai. When this one
came back, he told me that Mordecai basically
wanted me to go to the King and beg him to show
mercy to the Jews. So I sent a message straight
back to Mordecai, pointing out the problem with this
latest plan: The King has not asked to see me.

I explained that no one can just turn up to see the
King and expect to live, even me. The one exception
would be if, upon reaching the King, he held out
his gold sceptre. But who knows if he will do that
or not? Mordecai is basically asking me to risk
my life.

Mordecai refuses a gift.
Esther sends him some lovely clothes to wear.
But he prefers to wear sackcloth.
Itchy,
uncomfortable,
ugly
sackcloth.

In those days, people wore sackcloth as a sign of grief
or mourning.
Mordecai was grieving.
He was grieving the coming destruction of the Jews.
In a sense, Esther's gift was saying, 'Cheer up.
Change your clothes.
Don't wallow.'
And Mordecai says no.
He probably doesn't understand what's going on.
Possibly cannot fathom why God is allowing power to
someone like Haman.
Life is hard.
Everything is terrible.
I'm keeping my sackcloth, thank you very much.
So he sits there, wearing sackcloth.
When nice clothes are within his grasp.

What about you?
Are you determined to wear sackcloth when nice
clothes are there for the taking?

Isaiah 61:3 says God has given us a 'garment of praise instead of a spirit of despair'.
Nice clothes are there.
They're a God-gift.
But God can't force us to take them.
And so often, we don't.
We don't take them.
We choose despair above praise
rather than praise above despair.
We keep our sackcloth, thank you very much.
In righteous indignation, or stubbornness, or whatever it is,
we
cling
to
our
sackcloth.
And it's itchy and it's uncomfortable but we do it anyway,
turning our backs on what God offers.
Freedom.
Peace.
Assurance.
Ratification.
Reason.
Forgiveness.
And more.

Day 10

But what about when, like Mordecai, wearing
sackcloth is very legitimate?
When tough things hit us left, right and centre?
When life is hard?
When everything does seem terrible?

Well, we don't deny our sackcloth times.
We don't pretend they don't exist,
in pseudo-triumph.
It's OK to say to God,
'I'm covered in sackcloth.
Legitimately.
Because life is hard right now.'
He hears.
And knows.
And cares.

Isaiah 43:2 (NLT):
'When you go through deep waters, I will be with you.'

And we do choose praise above despair.
'Above' can mean 'over'.
Choosing praise over despair.

Or 'above' can mean overhead.
Praise is 'overhead' our despair.
Despair is still there but is covered by praise.

71

Psalm 91:4 (NLT):

'He will cover you with his feathers. He will shelter you with his wings.'

Even in our sackcloth, we are covered and sheltered by God.

Overhead: positioned or coming from above.
The ability to praise in our darkest times comes from God.
God, who is overhead.

Ephesians 4:6:

'[O]ne God and Father of all, who is over all and through all and in all.'

Praise: the giving of thanks to a deity
And, no matter how great our despair, we can always say a thank you to God. 'Thank you that you're with me in this.'
Because he is.
Always.

Joshua 1:5:

'I will never leave you nor forsake you.'

God wants to be in things with you.
Rather than entering into God's presence being a sure way to risk your life,

it is a sure way to find security.
Even when life's hard.
And tears are
dripping
onto
your
sackcloth.

Habakkuk 3:17,18:
*'Though the fig-tree does not bud
and there are no grapes on the vines,
though the olive crop fails
and the fields produce no food,
though there are no sheep in the sheepfold
and no cattle in the stalls,
yet I will rejoice in the Lord,
I will be joyful in God my Saviour.'*

Father God,

*You're with me.
In everything.
Overhead.
All the time.
So I always have something to be thankful for.
Thank you.
Help praise to be 'overhead' my tough times.
'Yet I will be joyful in you . . .'*

Amen

Esther's Quest

Praise is overhead

My response:

Day 11

Mordecai doesn't give up, that's for sure! He has sent a message in reply, saying that if I do not speak out, my family will die. Help for the Jews will come from somewhere else in the end, but my family will die. And I think he's right about that; Haman is really on the warpath. Mordecai also asked me a question: Maybe I became Queen for such a time as this?

That really got me thinking. I have often wondered, why me? Why do I have so much? Maybe this is my answer.

Why?
Why me?
Why am I going through such a tough time?
Why do I have to risk my life,
my comfort,
my routine?
It's a common question, and one Esther could have asked.
And she did.
Esther did wonder 'why'.
As Elizabeth, when visited by Mary, asked 'why?'
(Luke 1:43).

Why . . . am I so blessed?
It's a good perspective.
As we go through life, it can be so easy to focus on the negatives.
To allow the tough times to overwhelm us.
But what if we choose not to?
What if, as the old hymn says, we choose to 'count our blessings' instead?
Look for the positives.
And hold on to them.
Tightly.

One of Esther's blessings was to become Queen.
To have a home, wealth, status . . .
But even being Queen didn't let her off the hook.
Didn't exempt her from the plight of others.
From the possibility of being sacrificially generous.

Sometimes, the more we have materially, the harder it is to be generous.
We saw that with the rich young ruler.

What do you do with what you have?

Why am I so blessed?

And what do you do with who you are?
Your skills/talents/position/time?

Why am I so blessed?

Day 11

Hebrews 13:16 (NLT):
'Don't forget to do good and to share with those in need. These are the sacrifices that please God.'

So, Mordecai asks Esther for help.
Again.

Let's look at a parable Jesus told in Luke 18:

Again and again, a woman is treated unfairly.
Apart from the fact that she is a widow, all we know about her is that she didn't give up.
Again and again she is mistreated.
And again and again she asks a notoriously unfair judge for help.
For support.
For justice.
And he says no.
Please?
'No.'
Please?
'No.'
Please?
Help me.
'No. I don't think so.'
Please?
'I'm getting tired of you. No.'
Please?
'Didn't you hear me? No.'
Please?

77

Please?

Please?

And in the end, worn down by her persistence, the judge says, 'Yes.'

Jesus told this parable to teach about prayer.

Basically: Don't stop praying.

Don't give up.

And don't forget that unlike the widow, you're not coming before injustice.

You're coming before the one who is called 'The Lord Our Righteousness' (Jeremiah 23:6, ISV).

You're coming before righteousness itself.

Isaiah 46:13:

'I am bringing my righteousness near.'

I'm bringing it near.

Because I want to.

Father God, help me?

Yes, my child.

Yes.

Yes.

Yes.

The widow didn't give up.

She kept asking the judge to help.

The only person who could.
Mordecai didn't give up.
He kept asking Esther to help.
The only person who could.
What about you?
Do you give up asking for help?
Or do you keep asking the only one who can?

Jeremiah 29:12:
'Call on me and come and pray to me, and I will listen to you.'

God put Esther in the right place at the right time.
And God, who ordained every day of your life (see Psalm 139:16), put you where you are.
Right now.
For 'such a time as this' (Esther 4:14).

Is he asking you to do something?
Esther was being asked to do something.

Or perhaps he has brought you to where you are so you can stop.
Perhaps he is asking you to simply be.
Rest.
Pray.
Mordecai, by the gate, was being asked to be.

Psalm 46:10:
'Be still, and know that I am God.'

The word 'know' here means 'understand'.
Spend time sitting by the gate of heaven.
Understanding that he is God.
You're not.
And you're not expected to be.

Father God, help me – please?
Yes, my child.
Yes.
Yes.
Yes.

Father God,

Help me to be still.
You are God.
Which means I'm not.
You know best.
Which means I don't.
You are righteous.
I'm not.
And yet I can come before righteousness itself.
Thank you that I'm so blessed.

Amen

Esther's Quest

Count my
blessings

My response:

Day 12

Oh, this is such a dilemma. Why is it me this is happening to? I would like to just run away, to be honest, but deep down I know that Mordecai is right. So it's not a dilemma really, I guess.

I've just sent a reply back to Mordecai telling him to ask all the Jews he can to fast for me. I and my maids will fast, too. Then, after three days of this, I will go to the King. I know I might die but if I do, I do.

How can I pray for you?
May I pray with you?
I'll pray for you.

In effect, that's what Esther was asking the people to say to her.
She needed their support.
So she asked for it.
She's been there for others – for example, when she saved the King from assassination:
'I'll be there for you.'
And now she needed other people to be there for her:
'Please be there for me.'

Which do you think was easier to say?

So often, as Christians, perhaps we are better at
giving help than receiving it.
We don't like asking for help.

Maybe that's because we don't like putting people out.
We don't want to burden anyone with our own
problems.

In Acts 20:35, we see Jesus himself said: 'It is more
blessed to give than to receive.'

By not asking for help from others, not asking them to
give support, could it be that we are actually denying
them a blessing?
We are not allowing others to be blessed through giving?
Preventing someone else from being blessed:
Is that what we're called to do?
No.

Maybe, independent as we are, asking for help does
not occur to us.
We're so used to surviving alone that it becomes
automatic.

What about with God?

Why is turning to God often a last resort, rather than a
first port of call?

Does asking him for help not occur to us?

Let's look at Naaman, 2 Kings 5:

Naaman is a commander of the Aram army.
And he has leprosy.
Fortunately for Naaman, he's been told of a man who can help him.
Elisha, the prophet.
So off he goes to Elisha's house, taking money as a gift.
And new clothes.
Armed with his gifts, he's done all he can.
And so he makes the journey to see Elisha.
Mile.
After mile.
After mile.
Eventually, Naaman arrives.
But Elisha doesn't want to see him.
In fact, he refuses to.
He sends a messenger instead.
Who tells Naaman to go and wash seven times in the river.
And he'll be healed.
The leprosy will be gone.
For good.
Great news for Naaman.
Except it wasn't.

Naaman is absolutely furious.
He expected Elisha to come,

call on the name of God,
wave his hands
and cure the leprosy.
But that's not what happened.
And Naaman is left standing amongst the gifts he's
brought.
Thoughts of things he thought Elisha would do.
Shattered expectations.
Facing the decision of whether to do the thing that
would not have occurred to him in a million years.
As a last resort, Naaman gives it a try.
Wash seven times in the river.
Namaan decides 'yes'.
And he's healed.

Is turning to God often a last resort for you?

Psalm 50:15:
*'Call on me in the day of trouble; I will deliver
you, and you will honour me.'*

'I will deliver you.'
I will help.
I will make your burdens lighter.

'And you will honour me.'
When we stop trying to go it alone,
when we turn to God,
when we pray to him,
when we look to him,

when we make him our first port of call
in any situation,
we don't only help ourselves.
We honour God.

So could it be that those times when we don't turn to
him, we are denying him honour?
If so, is that what we're called to do?
Deny God honour?
No, it's not.

And what could be better than honouring God?

He's always waiting.

Honour him by making him your first port of call.

Father God,

I've never really thought about it before.
By not asking for prayer,
I'm denying blessing to others?
By not praying to you when I'm in trouble,
I'm denying you honour?
I'm sorry.
I don't want to do either of those things.
Help me to have the courage to share my burdens.

Amen

Esther's Quest

Ask for prayer

My response:

Day 13

OK, so the three days are up now. It's time to go to the King. I didn't know that three days could pass so quickly! I've just spent ages getting ready. I am wearing my best perfume and my royal robes. I hope Xerxes will be pleased when he sees me.

Right, off I go. This may be my last diary entry ever . . .

(Later) I'm back and all is well! Xerxes saw me standing near his court and he held out his gold sceptre to me – he was pleased to see me after all.

Esther prepares herself.
Chooses her best clothes.
She wants to be the best that she can be.
And why?
Because she's going to enter the King's presence.
She'd been chosen by him and she wanted to wear what would please him.

What about us?
As we go before God, our King?
The one who chose us.
Do we wear what pleases him?

Day 13

Do we know what pleases him?
The Bible tells us:

Colossians 3:12:
*'Therefore, as God's chosen people, holy and dearly
loved, clothe yourselves with compassion, kindness,
humility, gentleness and patience.'*

Compassion: I care about what other people are
going through.
Kindness: I will do whatever I can to help.
Humility: I will not big myself up or make out that I'm
better than anyone else.
Gentleness: I will be loving towards people, however
they behave towards me.
Patience: Everything does not need to be done
yesterday. I will give people time.

And I will behave in a
compassionate,
kind,
humble,
gentle,
patient
way towards myself, as well.

Because I'm wearing those things.
They're covering me.
All the time.

So, unsure of her reception, Esther enters the King's
presence.
The King sees her standing there.
Esther's heart pounds.
Nervously.
And the King holds out his golden sceptre.
He is pleased to see her.

Let's look at Luke 15:

A man is walking down a dusty road.
He's been walking for a long time.
But that's not the only reason he looks so scruffy.
So dirty.
So bedraggled.
The rags on his back are all he owns.
Yes, he used to have money, friends, status.
But not anymore.
He'd wanted money so he could leave home.
So that's what his father gave him.
And the man frittered it all away.
Now, on that dusty road,
dirty and bedraggled,
hungry and tired,
despairing and alone,
there is only one thing he wants.
To see his dad.
Part of him is saying that there is no way his father
will ever want to see him.

Part of him, the part that persuades him to take step
after exhausting step, says:

But maybe he will.

Maybe.

Hopefully.

As he gets closer to home, the man's steps start to
drag.

He knows he's risking rejection.

Hurt.

Anger.

But he keeps going.

Because he wants to see his dad.

He just wants to see his dad.

He can't wear smart clothes.

Because he hasn't got any.

But he just wants to see his dad.

So he keeps going.

Despite the fact that he's only got the threadbare rags
he's wearing.

Rags which, all of a sudden, are hidden.

He can't see them anymore.

Because he is enveloped, rags and all, by a great big
bear hug.

From his dad.

His rags didn't matter.

All his dad cared about was that he'd come home.

His dad just wanted to be with him.

Whatever state his son was in.

He welcomed him.

And yes, he gave him new clothes.

We have a God who welcomes us, whatever state we are in.
Struggling.
Feeling dirty.
Resentful.
Worthless.
Whatever it may be.

He loves you.
And THEN he gives you new clothes.

Isaiah 51:15,16:

'I am the LORD your God . . . I have . . . covered you with the shadow of my hand.'

Father God,

Thank you that you meet me more than half way.
When I come to you, you never reject me.
You welcome me.
You cover all my shame with a heavenly hug, just for me.
And then you give me new clothes.
Help me remember to wear them.
To show compassion, kindness, gentleness, humility, patience.
Towards others.
And towards myself.

Amen

Esther's Quest

God gives me new
clothes

My response:

Day 14

The King asked me what I would like. He said he would give me anything, even half his kingdom.

Well, I wasn't thinking of asking for anything quite on that scale. I mean, what would I do with half a kingdom? I wouldn't know where to start! So I guess Xerxes might have been a bit surprised when I just asked that he and Haman come to a banquet later. But he immediately sent someone to invite Haman and Haman is on his way now – I'd better go and get ready.

What would you like?

That's what Xerxes wanted to know.

Let's look at Solomon, 2 Chronicles 1:

Solomon is King of Israel.
He's a good king.
A great king.
He's established the kingdom well.
Because God is with him.

Day 14

One day, the entire nation gets together and they all
worship God.
Solomon offers 1,000 burnt offerings.
Extravagant worship.
Then everyone goes home.
And then something else happens to Solomon.
That same night, God appears to him.
And God has a question.
'What would you like me to give you?'

Let's pause here for a minute.
God asks Solomon, 'What would you like me to give
you?'
Think about it.
'What would you like me to give you?'
What would you say?
As you look at your life,
your needs,
your desires,
your wants,
what would your answer be?

'What would you like me to give you?'

God has asked Solomon a question.
And he's waiting for an answer.
Solomon gives one.
He points out that God made him king.
That's the only reason he's king at all.

And then he makes his request.
'Give me wisdom to govern.'
Help me to be king.
Help me do the job you gave me.
Help me be the person you want me to be.

We should all be like Solomon.
Asking God to help us be the people he wants us to be.
Day by day.
Minute by minute.
Asking for strength.
For discernment.
For wisdom to live every situation as God would want.

God was pleased with Solomon's request.
And he said yes.
More than yes.
He added other blessings beside.
God has a habit of doing that.
Adding blessings beside.
When we truly live as he wants us to, the blessings
keep coming.

John 1:16 (NLT):
*'From his abundance we have all received one gracious
blessing after another.'*

Perhaps Xerxes was surprised when Esther turned
down his offer of half the kingdom.

It was a pretty huge thing to be offered.
And yet she turned it down.
She actually said no to what the king was offering.
Seems ludicrous, doesn't it.
Or does it?

How often do we do the same?
God offers peace, security, acceptance, love,
belonging etc. etc.
Do we turn it down?

Luke 13:34:

*'Jerusalem, Jerusalem, you who kill the prophets and
stone those sent to you, how often I have longed to
gather your children together, as a hen gathers her
chicks under her wings, and you were not willing.'*

Jesus said this.
People were rejecting help.
From people sent to them.
And from Jesus himself.
Even though he was right there.
Right there.
Essentially saying,
'I'll protect you.
I'll help you.
I'll shield you.
I'll love you.
I'll give you the best.'

And people were not willing to take him up on it. They said no.

Do you say no to what your King offers?

Choosing, instead, to live your life hoping for what you could have?

Hoping for what is actually yours already.

Ephesians 1:3:
'Praise be to the God and Father of our Lord Jesus Christ, who has blessed us'.

Father God,

What would I like?
I'd like to be the person you want me to be.
Give me wisdom to know how you want me to live.
To live the life you've given me.
And to remember that you are always there.
Enabling me, every step of the way.
I can't do it on my own.
Thank you that you never ask me to.

Amen

Esther's Quest

What would I like?

My response:

Day 15

The banquet went well, I think. The King and Haman both arrived for it in good spirits and they enjoyed the food and wine. At least I assume they did, judging by the amount that they managed to put away between them!

At one point, Xerxes asked me again what my request was, and again he promised me anything up to half his kingdom. But I still need more time so I told him that if they both came back for another banquet tomorrow, I would tell him my request then.

'There's more to come.'

That's what Esther says to Haman and Xerxes.
They've finished their meal.
Presumably they enjoyed it.
But the conversation hadn't really got beyond small talk.
Perhaps they were wondering why the two of them had been invited, together, to dine with the Queen?
Just them.

Surely Esther hadn't gone to all this effort just to make small talk?

'There's more to come.'

Wait for it.
Don't go too far away.
Stick around until I'm ready to tell you.
When I'm ready.
In my timing.

Let's look at the Mount of Transfiguration, Matthew 17:

Peter is walking up a mountain.
So is John.
And James.
Leading the way is Jesus.

Jesus led them up the mountain.
He didn't say, 'Go and figure it out for yourselves.'
He said, 'Follow me.'

Psalm 23:1–2
'The Lord is my shepherd, I lack nothing . . . he leads me.'

When we follow our Shepherd,
whether he leads us up a mountain,
beside quiet waters,

through a storm,
down a long, winding road,
we
lack
nothing.
Because he's there, too.

The disciples had been so excited when they set off.
Out of everyone, Jesus had picked them.
Just the three of them to climb the mountain with him.
At first, it was easy walking.
Then the mountain got steeper.
And steeper.
They were really climbing now.
Out of breath.
Trying to keep going.
And still they didn't know exactly where they were going.
Or why.
Jesus hadn't told them.
But he kept leading them higher.
Higher.
Higher.
And they followed.
They may have huffed and puffed, but they stayed with him.
Perhaps they asked him where they were going.
Perhaps they didn't.
Either way, Jesus kept going.
And they stuck with him.

Day 15

'There's more to come.'

They believed, despite the struggle, it would be
worth it.
And then, there were no more questions.
Because Jesus was transfigured before their very eyes.
He was transformed.
His face shone like the sun.
His clothes were dazzling white.
And then, as if that weren't enough, they heard the
voice of God.
'This is my Son.
I love him.
I'm pleased with him.
Listen to him.'

The trudge up the mountain, the sore feet, the
questions . . . all were forgotten.
No wheres.
No whys.
Because they knew the answer.
God had spoken directly to them.
In his timing, the disciples experienced something
amazing.

'There's more to come.'

The disciples were reminded of who Jesus was.
It's a good thing to be reminded of.

Perhaps living with Jesus every day caused the disciples to become complacent.
To forget just who it was that they spent their days with.

What about you?
Does familiarity cause you to forget who it is you have the privilege of living life with?
Remind yourself:

Colossians 1:15–20 (NLT):

'Christ is the visible image of the invisible God.
He existed before anything was created
and is supreme over all creation,
for through him God created everything
in the heavenly realms and on earth.
He made the things we can see
and the things we can't see –
such as thrones, kingdoms, rulers, and authorities in the unseen world.
Everything was created through him and for him.
He existed before anything else,
and he holds all creation together.
Christ is also the head of the church,
which is his body.
He is the beginning,
supreme over all who rise from the dead.
So he is first in everything.
For God in all his fullness

Day 15

*was pleased to live in Christ,
and through him God reconciled
everything to himself.
He made peace with everything in heaven and on earth
by means of Christ's blood on the cross.'*

Wow.

Stick around.
'There's more to come.'

Psalm 77:19:
*'Your path led through the sea, your way through the
mighty waters, though your footprints were not seen.'*

Follow his path.
Even if the details are not clear.
Stick with God.
Keep following.
He'll tell you.
When he's ready.
Wait for it:
'There's more to come.'

1 Corinthians 2:9 (NLT):
*'No eye has seen, no ear has heard,
and no mind has imagined what God
has prepared for those who love him.'*

Father God,

I have a confession.
I am not always very good at waiting.
But then, you know that.
Help me to trust in your timing.
To stick around.
To remember who I'm following.
I know there's more to come.
Help me to be in the right place when it does.

Amen

Esther's Quest

There's more to come

My response:

Day 16

Haman was really happy when he left the palace earlier. Fair enough, I suppose; not everyone gets to eat with the King and Queen two days running!

But, as I found out from Mordecai later, Haman did not stay happy for long. As he left, he had to pass by the place where Mordecai sits. And of course, Mordecai did not show Haman any sign of reverence at all. Apparently, Haman's face was like thunder when he saw this. He turned towards Mordecai but he did manage to pull himself together and leave before doing any damage. But for how long? I am worried about what will happen to Mordecai . . .

Let's look at a story in Mark 14:

It takes place in a man's home.
Simon's house.
There's a dinner party being held.
Everyone is celebrating.

And who has been invited as the guest of honour?
Jesus.

What about you?
As you go about your life,
whatever circumstances come your way,
do you invite Jesus to be part of it?
More than part of it.
To be the guest of honour?

So, all the guests are relaxing round the table.
When a woman appears.
Carrying an alabaster jar of expensive perfume.

She goes to Jesus,
breaks the jar
and pours the perfume on his head.

Seeing this, the guests start muttering to themselves.
What's she doing?
What a waste of money:
that perfume is expensive.
The money could have been given to the poor.

They stop muttering.
And they start speaking harshly.
They turn on the woman.
Having a go at her.

But Jesus steps in.
'Leave. Her. Alone.'

To the guests, the woman was not behaving as she should.
She was not fitting in with their notion of what was proper.
Which made them angry.

Just as Mordecai was not behaving as Haman thought he should.
Which made Haman angry.

But Mordecai and the woman have something in common.
They put Someone Else before people.

Luke 4:8 (NLT):
'You must worship the LORD your God and serve only him.'

He's the one that mattered.
He's the one that matters.
Does he matter to you?
Enough to put him first?

Mordecai and the woman wanted what was right.

That's why Mordecai refused to bow down to Haman.
That's why the woman was sacrificial in what she gave to Jesus.

She risked money.
She risked ridicule.
And yet she gave.
Giving to Jesus made her life more difficult in some ways.
Made it hurt.
Yet she gave.

And Jesus said,
'She has done a beautiful thing to me' (Mark 14:6).

A beautiful thing.
She'd taken what was possibly the most precious, valuable thing she owned.
The perfume was very expensive.
Yet it was worth nothing in comparison to being able to do something special for Jesus.
So she poured it over his head.
Anointing him.
Worshipping him.

Giving from the heart is beautiful.
Even when it hurts.

Jesus said,
'She has done a beautiful thing to me.'

But the guests didn't agree.
She was not fitting into their mould.

She wasn't behaving as they thought she should.

And so they got angry.

How do we react when people behave differently
from us in front of God?
Do we get angry?
Or are we able to consider the possibility that their
way of being may actually be – well – worship?
Doing 'a beautiful thing' for the one who matters.
For Jesus.

One of the guests, and one of Jesus' disciples, Judas
Iscariot, was angry.
So angry that he went off in a rage.

He missed out on a beautiful thing:
Sharing in the lives and joy of others.
He could have shared in the happiness that this
woman's worship brought Jesus.
But he didn't.
Because he was angry.
Things weren't as he wanted them to be.
So he went off on his own.
Away from life.
And he let anger be stronger than happiness.

Do you do that?
Allow anger to be stronger than happiness in your life?

Ecclesiastes 7:9 (NLT):
'Control your temper, for anger labels you a fool.'

When things aren't as you'd like them to be,
are you like Judas?
Finding foolishness in anger?
Or are you like the woman?
Finding worth in worship?

And Jesus said,
'She has done a beautiful thing to me.'

> *Father God,*
>
> *Sometimes people want to do things differently.*
> *Help me to remember that's OK.*
> *Different does not have to mean wrong.*
> *Thank you that you are a God of individuals.*
> *You love to receive our worship, whatever form it takes.*
> *Help me to join in your happiness when other people do 'beautiful things' for you.*
> *Help me to do beautiful things, too.*
>
> *Amen*

Esther's Quest

Don't let anger beat happiness

My response:

Day 17

It looks as though I was right to be concerned about Mordecai. It seems that Haman went home and threw a party. He boasted to all his friends about his great wealth and fine family and recent promotion, and how he was the only one who I'd invited to the banquets along with the King. To be fair, I imagine people were quite impressed at this list. But Haman told them that there was one thing that was stopping him from enjoying all this. And that one thing was Mordecai.

Haman's wife and friends told him to have some gallows built and get the King's permission to hang Mordecai on them in the morning. Then he would be able to properly enjoy the banquet later that day. Haman is putting this plan into action and the gallows are being built right now. I'm not sure what to do. In fact, I'm not sure that there is anything I can do.

Haman's life is looking pretty good right now.
He has a lot to celebrate.
But he's not.
He's not celebrating it.

Because there is one thing that is not so good.
And that's the thing that dominates everything else.
Mordecai.
Let's look at Hannah, 1 Samuel 1:

Hannah has a comfortable life.
Her husband is a man of wealth and position.[1]
He cares about Hannah.
A lot.
In fact, although he has another wife, Hannah is his favourite.
By a long way.
So, Hannah is cared for.
She is loved.
She wants for nothing.
Except one thing.
There is one negative in her seemingly idyllic life.
And that's the thing that dominates everything else.
Hannah longs to have a child.
Year after year goes by.
Still no child.
And it becomes all-consuming for Hannah.

What she's not got is all she can think about.
Similar to Haman.
But there the similarity ends.

Haman decides to take it upon himself.
Hannah decides to take it to God.

She prays.
And prays.
And prays.
In the end, Hannah does have a child.
God grants her that.
But the point is, she didn't know he would.
And still she prayed.
She took that big negative in her life and she said,
'OK, God, I'm finding this hard.
Really hard.
I can't deal with it.
I just can't.
But I can talk to you.'

Are you a Haman or a Hannah?
Taking responsibility for dealing with tough stuff
upon yourself?
Or taking that responsibility and giving it to God?

1 Peter 5:7:
'Cast all your anxiety on him because he cares for you.'

God cares for you.
The God who made the entire world.
Cares for you.
The God who knows all there is to know.
Cares for you.
The God who never sleeps.
Cares for you.

The God who listens.
Cares for you.
The God who can deal with things.
Cares for you.

That's why you can cast all your anxiety on him.
Because he cares for you.
He really does.

Haman realized that he was feeling negative.
And that his negativity needed dealing with.
He went the wrong way about it.
But he recognized that something needed to be done.
For Haman, dealing with it meant getting rid of it.

Sometimes, we do need to get rid of things.
Things in our lives that stop us living as God wants us to.
Things that take his place.

Colossians 3:5 (NLT):

'So put to death the sinful, earthly things lurking within you. Have nothing to do with sexual immorality, impurity, lust, and evil desires. Don't be greedy, for a greedy person is an idolater, worshiping the things of this world.'

Some things in our lives need dealing with.
Need working through.
Others need to go.

Father God,

I have a habit of taking too much upon myself.
Of thinking that I need to deal with things.
Especially things I think need changing for the better.
Help me to bring my negatives to you.
Again and again if I need to.
You share my pain.
My heartache.
Yet I stubbornly try to stop you sharing it.
By trying to deal with it myself.
Help me remember that I don't need to do that.
Ever.
Thank you that you care for me.

Amen

Esther's Quest

What do I do with
my negatives?

My response:

Day 18

Or maybe I don't need to do anything! The King has sorted it out. Last night, Xerxes couldn't sleep so he asked for the official records of his reign to be brought and read to him. When he heard the bit about Mordecai exposing the assassination plot, he wanted to know what honour Mordecai had received. Of course, the answer was 'none' and so Xerxes demanded to know who was in the court right then. Well, Haman was, as he'd just arrived to ask the King about hanging Mordecai.

So Haman was brought before Xerxes and asked what he thought should be done for the man that the King wanted to honour. Haman thought the King must be talking about Haman himself. After all, wasn't he a favourite with the King? So he said that the man should be given royal robes and led on one of the King's own horses through the city, with someone going in front shouting that this was what was done for the man the King delighted to honour.

'Great idea,' said Xerxes, and sent Haman off to do exactly that for Mordecai!

Let's look at Luke 17:

Ten men are standing in a group.
Suddenly they see Jesus coming.
They go to meet him.
But they don't get too close.
For a reason.
Each one of these men has leprosy.
They're disfigured.
They're contagious.
Outcasts.
Keeping their distance from people is normal.
They do it all the time.
So they automatically stop.
Before they get too close.
Putting up barriers.
Even with Jesus.

What about you?
Do you put up barriers?
Keep your distance?
Not let people get too close?
Not let Jesus get too close?

Well, thankfully, Jesus is good at crossing barriers:

Ephesians 2:13:
*'But now in Christ Jesus you who once were far away
have been brought near by the blood of Christ.'*

You were far away from God.
And maybe you still feel far away from God.

Remember: Through his death, Jesus crossed a barrier
for you.
A distance-barrier you couldn't cross.
So he crossed it instead.
By hanging on the cross.
He closed the distance-gap.
Actually, he destroyed the distance-gap.
Which means there's nothing in the way of you
coming to him.

Don't keep Jesus at arm's length.

So there they are.
A group of men, rejected by society, unwanted, left
to rot.
And yet, somehow, they find courage to draw near.
Across the gap.
Across the distance they're forced to keep.
In the only way they can.
They call out.

'Come near to God' ...

'Have pity on us!'
That's all they say.
They've reached rock bottom.

And they need someone to care.
To see them as people, not rejects.
'Have pity on us!'
Please?

... *'and he will come near to you' (James 4:8).*

The Ephesians passage goes on to say: 'He himself is
[your] peace.'

So, when peace seems further away than ever,
come near to Jesus.
To peace.
And he – peace – will come near to you.

Jesus sees the men.
And he answers:
'Go to the priests.'
So the men go.
And, as they do, they are healed.
No more leprosy.

One of them looks down.
Perhaps at his arms, his legs, his hands ...
Smooth as anything.
And his heart overflows with gratitude.

He dashes back to Jesus,
falls on his knees and shouts:

Day 18

'Thank you!
Thank you so much.'

One man.
He's a lone voice.
Where are the others?

So often, gratitude gets forgotten.
Thank you is bypassed.

Xerxes forgot.
He forgot to thank Mordecai.
The nine men forgot, too.
But, unlike Xerxes, their forgetting was permanent.

Do you forget to thank God?
Bypass thank you?

In every day, there is something to be thankful for.

And it's never too late.

Psalm 107:1:
*'Give thanks to the LORD, for he is good; his love endures
for ever.'*

What will you be thankful for today?

Father God,

Thank you for . . . .
And, thank you.

Amen

Esther's Quest

thank you

My response:

Day 19

I saw the whole thing and I almost felt sorry for Haman.

Haman went to Mordecai and explained what was happening (ungraciously!). Mordecai looked very surprised but in the end realized that Haman looked far too miserable to be joking, so allowed him to put the robe around Mordecai's shoulders. Then Mordecai climbed on to the horse and off they went, with Haman shouting that this was what was done for the man the King delighted to honour. Xerxes had been very specific about Haman carrying out his own recommendations to the letter. Afterwards, Haman rushed home and shared his grief and humiliation with his wife.

But Mordecai returned to his usual place at the King's Gate.

Mordecai is sitting by the gate.
As usual.
When, suddenly, Haman appears.
Unusually, Haman is not expecting to be bowed down to.

Instead, he gestures for Mordecai to climb on to his horse.

'Do to others what you would have them do to you' (Matthew 7:12).

Well, this is certainly what Haman ended up doing.
Here was someone he'd wanted to be honoured by.
Someone he thought he deserved honour from.
But someone who, instead, he's forced to honour.
Unwillingly.
Begrudgingly.
He did it.
But only because he had no choice.
Basically, Haman did it with the wrong attitude.
He was well aware of the great honour bestowed on Mordecai.
After all, he'd wanted to be the one riding that horse.
Haman couldn't be pleased for Mordecai.
Because he was jealous.
In some ways, that seems strange.

Haman was the King's right-hand man.
He had wealth and privilege galore.
He ate at the King's table.
Mordecai, on the other hand, spent his days by the King's Gate.
Sitting in the dust.

Yet Haman wanted more.
His jealousy prevented him from being happy for
other people.
More.
And so his jealousy prevented him from being happy
at all.
He wanted more.
More.

Let's look at a parable Jesus told, Luke 12:

A farmer is doing well.
He is rich.
He is comfortable.
And, to cap it all off, this year his crops do well.
Really well.
'Fantastic,' says the farmer.
'I have lots to share.'

Except he didn't.
He didn't say that.
He said, 'Oh, no.
What shall I do?
I have no room to store all my crops.'
Then he realizes.
He doesn't need to store all the extra crops for
himself.
He already has plenty.
So he will share, after all.

Except he doesn't.
He doesn't realize that:
'I know.
If I tear down my barns
and build bigger ones
I can keep all my crops in there.
For myself.
I'll be set for life!'

And God says to him,
'You fool.'
Your priorities are wrong.
You.
Self-interested.
Fool.

The man died that night.
As God had always known he would.
The farmer was not able to enjoy what he'd saved.
And his greed had prevented him from being happy
while he lived.
Like Haman.
His priorities were wrong.
You.
Fool.

What about your priorities?
How full of self-interest are they?
Don't be a fool.

'Do to others what you would have them do to you'
(Matthew 7:12).

Haman was a fool.
He got his priorities wrong.
He should have been happy to share in the
unexpected celebration of Mordecai.
But he wasn't.

Was Mordecai happy about being celebrated?
Well, he didn't refuse to climb on the horse.
Or wear the robe.
So presumably he didn't mind too much.
Perhaps he even enjoyed it.
But, when it was over, what did he do?
He returned to his usual place.
By the gate.
Mordecai didn't allow self-interest to control him.
His 'usual place' was where God wanted him to be.
And that was enough for him.
Haman's usual place was with the King.
But that wasn't enough for him.
He wanted more.
Self-interest got in the way.
He tried to give himself even more honour.
And it backfired.
You fool.

Matthew 23:12 (NLT):
'But those who exalt themselves will be humbled, and those who humble themselves will be exalted.'

Father God,

Sometimes, I'm not very nice.
Well, more than sometimes.
I become self-interested.
I get my priorities wrong.
I do want to be interested in the 'self' of others, too.
But it's hard.
I get jealous.
Even when I don't really know why.
And I prevent myself from being happy.
I'm a fool.
Please help me to let you lift me up.
When I try to lift myself, it doesn't work.

Amen

Esther's Quest

Don't be a fool

My response:

Day 20

Haman was still talking with his wife when people arrived to bring him to my banquet. To be fair to him, he managed to rally quite well and was in good spirits at the meal.

The King asked me again what my request was, and this time I knew I could put it off no longer. I had to speak out. I told him that my people had been sentenced to death.

Xerxes was furious and demanded to know who by. And the answer was one word: Haman. The King was so angry that he got up and went out into the garden. I thought Haman would leave, too, as no man but the King is permitted to be alone with the Queen, but he didn't. Instead, he sat down next to me on the couch, begging me to save his life.

Then the King came back and found Haman on the couch with me and that was the last straw. Xerxes was fuming.

Esther is really worried.
She's hurting.
Her heart is breaking.
Because of a death sentence.
Her people's.
And maybe,

probably,
her own.

Rewind to when Esther appeared, uninvited, before
the King.
She faced death then.
And the thought of dying terrified her.

But this time it seems that her concerns are for others
above herself.
'My people have been sentenced to death.'

1 Corinthians 12:26:
'If one part suffers, every part suffers with it.'

Do you hurt when people hurt?
Do you allow others to hurt with you when you hurt?
Do you allow God to hurt with you when you hurt?

Let's look at John 11:

Mary and Martha's brother, Lazarus, is ill.
Jesus is one of their best friends.
He loves them.
They know he does.
And so they ask him to come.
He'll be able to fix this.
But he doesn't come when they want him to.
Or the way they told him to.
And Lazarus dies.

When Jesus does come, he sees Mary.
Crying.
His heart breaks.
And do you know what he does?
He doesn't pretend not to notice her tears.
He doesn't tell her to snap out of it.
He doesn't tell her to cheer up; everything will be OK.
He walks with her.
To the grave of her brother.

And there, standing with Mary in
her hurt,
Jesus weeps.
He cries her tears with her.
More than that, he cries shared tears.
Because her hurting is his hurting.

He'll cry shared tears with you, too.
He hurts when you hurt.
And if you allow him to walk with you to your
heartache,
he'll stand with you in your hurt.

John 11:35:
'Jesus wept.'

So, Haman acts unwisely.
When left alone with the Queen, protocol dictated
that he should walk away.
But he didn't.

Not only that but he sat down right next to the very person he should have been walking from.

Sometimes, we need to walk away.
We find ourselves in situations that, tempting though they may be, are:
Unhelpful.
Unwise.
Unedifying.
Ungodly.
And we need to walk away.

But, so often we don't.
We go to that situation and we sit right down beside it.

James 4:7:
'Submit yourselves, then, to God. Resist the devil, and he will flee from you.'

Ignoring protocol led to Haman behaving wrongly in front of royalty.

If we ignore God's protocol,
his guidance on how to live,
we'll be like Haman.

Acting unwisely.
Very unwisely.
Behaving wrongly in front of royalty.

And we are in the presence of royalty.
In the presence of God, our King.
All the time.

Joshua 1:9 (NLT):
'The LORD your God is with you wherever you go.'

And so everything we do is 'behaving in front of royalty'.
All the time.

Ephesians 5:10:
'Find out what pleases the Lord.'

Find out what behaviour pleases God.
And do it.

Father God,

You enter my heartache.
You share my hurting.
You cry my tears.
Thank you.

Amen

Esther's Quest

I live with royalty

My response:

Day 21

Xerxes was furious with Haman. One of Xerxes' assistants told him that Haman had built some gallows, intending to hang Mordecai. Xerxes immediately ordered that Haman be hanged on the gallows instead.

This has all happened so fast I can hardly take it in; I think I am in shock. I hoped Xerxes would listen to me but he did more than that, he supported me. But he was livid about what happened. In fact, it wasn't until Haman had been hanged that Xerxes managed to calm down and stop being angry.

2 Chronicles 7:12:
'The LORD appeared . . . and said: "I have heard your prayer."'

When we come to God in prayer, he listens.
We can be assured of that.
But what about support?
Do you believe that the God who listens to you is also a God who supports you?
Helps you?
Walks with you?

Ratifies you?
Encourages you?

Support: to take the weight of something, to prevent something from falling or sinking.

Let's look at Exodus 17:

Moses is standing at the top of a hill.
He has a stick in his hands.
The staff of God.
His hands are raised up high.
Further down the hill is the Israelite army.
Fighting.
When Moses' hands are held high, the army are winning.
But, if Moses gets tired,
and his hands start to droop,
the Israelite army begins to lose.

Moses does get tired.
And it's at that point that someone says,
'Moses, sit down.'
But surely there is nowhere to sit?
'Yes there is.
Because we've brought a stone for you to rest on.
Sit down.'
So Moses sits.
On the rock.

His legs are less tired now, but his arms still droop.
And they need to be held high.
Or the army will lose.
So Aaron stands on one side of Moses as he sits on the rock.
Hur stands on the other.
And the two of them hold Moses' hands high for him.
And the army wins.

They won because Aaron and Hur supported Moses.
And they won because Moses allowed himself to be supported.
He didn't refuse to sit on the rock.
He didn't snatch his hands away.
He stayed.
Surrounded by support.

What about you?
Do you rest on the Rock God offers you?
Allow him to support you?

Isaiah 26:4 (ISV):
'Trust in the LORD forever, for in the LORD God you have an everlasting rock.'

Or do you forget that you're surrounded by support?
And stand alone at the top of the hill.
Trying to win battles in your own strength.

Snatching your hands away.
Even when God says,
'Here, sit down.'
And offers to hold up your tired hands.

Matthew 11:28:
*'Come to me, all you who are weary and burdened,
and I will give you rest.'*

After the battle, Moses built an altar to God.
An altar he called 'The LORD is my Banner'.
Moses didn't only allow others to support him.
He acknowledged their support.
Hands were lifted up.
Not 'My hands stayed up, so we won'.
Hands were lifted up.
In other words, 'It's not all about me'.

Everyone had a part to play in this victory.
Those who fought.
Those who held Moses' hands up.
Moses, who sat on a rock.

1 Corinthians 3:5,6 (NLT):
*'After all, who is Apollos? Who is Paul? We are only God's
servants through whom you believed the Good News.
Each of us did the work the Lord gave us. I planted the
seed in your hearts, and Apollos watered it, but it was
God who made it grow.'*

'Each of us did the work God gave us.'
And God gave each of us something different
to do.
Different.
But equally important.

1 Corinthians 12:27 (NLT):
*'All of you together are Christ's body,
and each of you is a part of it.'*

Each of you is a part of it.
And that includes you.
Maybe you think that what you do is small.
Is insignificant.
Doesn't matter.

Maybe you think you are small.
Insignificant.
Don't matter.

Remember that you are part of the body of Christ.
If you weren't here, there'd be something missing.
Something vital.
Something valued.

Whether you are 'fighting'.
Out on the field.
In the thick of it.
Preaching, teaching, leading worship.

Whether you are 'holding people's hands up'.
Supporting people.
Helping them.
Praying for them.
Enabling them to do their God-given jobs.

Whether you are sitting on the rock.
Spending time resting in God.
Allowing others to support you.
Because you can't do it on your own.
And no one is asking you to.

Whatever you do, it matters.
And you matter.

'All of you together are Christ's body, and each of you
is a part of it.'

So, Xerxes is furious.
He's livid with Haman.
How dare Haman abuse his position like that?
And with Xerxes' own wife.
The audacity of the man.
The presumption.
What a nerve.
Haman is hanged for what he did.
And that's when Xerxes begins to be able to calm
down.
The issue has been dealt with.
And Xerxes is able to move on.

Day 21

Ephesians 4:26 (NLT):
'Don't let the sun go down while you are still angry.'

Deal with things.
Come before God.
Sit down on the Rock.
Let him hold you.
Let him support you.
Let him be there for you.
And you'll win your battles . . .

Father God,

When I am weak, you are strong.
Help me to live surrounded by support.
The best support.
Always.
When you say, 'Here, sit down.'
Let my answer be, 'Yes, please.'

Amen

Esther's Quest

Sit on the Rock

My response:

Day 22

The same day as Haman was hanged, Xerxes gave Haman's whole estate to me! He also met Mordecai, because I told him that Mordecai was related to me. And Xerxes gave Mordecai his own signet ring, as he'd previously given to Haman.

But I knew that just because the King had been angry with Haman, it didn't mean that he would answer my request. So I had to go to him again. I plucked up courage but when I got there, all I could do was fall on my knees and cry. In the end I managed to speak and ask him to put an end to what Haman had been planning to do to the Jews.

To be honest, I was so upset that I can't remember much about what happened but I do know this: the King held out his golden sceptre to me again and I got up and stood before him.

Esther knows what she needs to do.
She needs to go to the King.
Again.
And make a request of him.
Again.
So she plucks up her courage.

Again.
But, when she gets to Xerxes,
her pre-prepared words,
her 'holding it all together',
her strength;
they just disappear.
And Esther collapses at the King's feet.
Crying.

Let's look at a woman in Luke 7:

All we know about this woman is that she had 'lived a
sinful life'.
One day, she heard that Jesus was nearby.
More than that, she learned exactly where he was.
So off she went.
To the place where she knew Jesus was.
When she got there, she didn't speak.
She did not say a word to Jesus.
She went right up to him,
stood beside him,
and cried.
Maybe words were beyond her.
Maybe she didn't know what to say.
Maybe her situation was just so big that she didn't
know where to start.
But she went anyway.
She went to Jesus.
And she cried.

Day 22

Sometimes, life can be like that.
Overwhelming.
We don't know what to do.
Or say.
Or think.

In the midst of our not knowing, let's remember what
we do know.
We know Jesus is there.

Like the woman, we don't need words.
We can go to him.
Stay with him.
And cry.
Just cry.
And that's OK.

What does Xerxes do when he sees Esther, weeping
before him?
Well, he lets her cry.
And then he holds out his golden sceptre to her.
In her dishevelled,
tear-stained,
eyes swollen from crying,
wordless state,
he holds out the sceptre:
'I'm glad you're here.'

Just as Jesus says about the woman:
'I'm glad she's here.'

Just as he says to you,
'I'm glad you're here.'

Always.
Come.
Just come.
I'm glad you're here.

You wouldn't be if you knew what I'm like.
I'm glad you're here.
But I've really let you down.
I'm glad you're here.
I've had bad thoughts.
I'm glad you're here.
And I've enjoyed having bad thoughts.
I'm glad you're here.
I've been really grumbling.
I'm glad you're here.
I've done some terrible things.
I'm glad you're here.
I was mean to someone.
I'm glad you're here.
I've not made enough time for you.
I'm glad you're here.
But you can't be glad, because . . .
Stop.

Day 22

Just stop.
I do know what you're like.
And I'm glad you're here.

Father God,

When everything falls apart,
and I don't know what to do,
or say,
or think,
help me to remember what I do know:
You're there.
Waiting for me.
And, in whatever state I arrive,
you always say:
'I'm glad you're here.'

Amen

Esther's Quest

Jesus is glad I'm here

My response:

Day 23

As I stood before the King, suddenly I felt calm. He had allowed me to stand there so he must be at least willing to listen.

I asked him if he held me in high regard and if he felt it was the right thing to do, to please change the order that Haman had given about destroying all the Jews. I told him that I couldn't bear to see the destruction of my people, of my family.

Let's look at Elijah, 1 Kings 17:

Elijah is a house-guest of a woman and her son.
They've let him stay in their spare room.
They don't have much food to spare but, what they do have, they share with Elijah.
And then, one day, the son becomes ill.
Really ill.
In fact, he dies.
And the woman is furious with Elijah.
She blames him.
And she tells him so.

Elijah looks at her as she rages.
As she yells at him.

As she accuses him.
And he is filled with compassion.
He sees beyond her words into her heartache.
She's hurting.
And Elijah wants to help.
'Give me your son.'
Elijah takes the boy upstairs to his own room and lays him on his bed.
Then he prays.
And God brings the boy back to life.

Elijah couldn't bear to see the destruction of this little family.
To see the woman hurting.
What about us?
As we look at people around us?
Our spiritual family?
Our brothers and sisters in Christ?
Do we see them?
Really see them?
Or don't we care enough to look?
Really look?
To see beyond their words into their heartache.
To see beyond the 'I'm fine, thanks' to the hurt that may lie beneath.
And, when we do see, do we take time to care?

Carrying the boy upstairs would have taken effort on Elijah's part.
Yet he did it.

And when he'd carried him to the top of the stairs,
as far as he could,
he laid him down.
On Elijah's own bed.
He laid him down.
But kept him close.

Sometimes, when we've cared enough to see beyond
'I'm fine',
and when we've done what we can to help people,
we need to lay them down.
Keep them close, yes.
But let go of trying to do things in our own strength.
Follow Elijah's example.
Let go.
Stay close.
And pray.

Elijah prayed.
Then he stayed close by stretching himself out beside
the boy – three times.
And then he prayed again.
In other words, he brought his worries to God more
than once.
As Esther brought her concerns for her people to
Xerxes more than once.

God doesn't mind how many times you come to him
and talk over the same worry.
Or concern.

Or problem.
If it's hurting you, he wants to know.
And he wants you to tell him.

Do you know why he wants you to tell him?
Because he cares.

1 Peter 5:7 (NLT):
'Give all your worries and cares to God, for he cares about you.'

Father God,

Thank you that you care.
Really care.
Sometimes I say 'I'm fine' when I'm not.
Even to you.
But you know that.
You see right through it.
Because you care.
Help me to follow your example
and care for others.

Amen

Esther's Quest

Really see

My response:

Day 24

And the King said OK! He told Mordecai and myself to write a new decree in his own name on behalf of the Jews. We are to seal it with Xerxes' own signet ring so that the words in the document can't be changed.

King Xerxes made sure that there was no way the words could be changed.
The document was sealed with his own seal.

You know, God writes words onto your heart.
And seals them himself.
So that they can't be changed.
No matter what.
Let's look at some:

Peace:
John 14:27: 'Peace I leave with you; my peace I give you.'
No matter what.

Courage:
Philippians 4:13 (NLT): 'For I can do everything through Christ, who gives me strength.'
No matter what.

Security:
John 10:29: 'No one can snatch [you] out of [God's] hand.'
No matter what.

Partnership:
Matthew 11:29 (NLT): 'Take my yoke upon you. Let me teach you, because I am humble and gentle at heart, and you will find rest for your souls.'
No matter what.

Refuge:
Psalm 61:2 (NLT): 'I cry to you for help when my heart is overwhelmed. Lead me to the towering rock of safety.'
No matter what.

A Clean Slate:
Lamentation 3:23 (NLT): 'Great is [God's] faithfulness; his mercies begin afresh each morning.'
No matter what.

Value:
Isaiah 43:4 (NLT): 'You are precious to me. You are honored, and I love you.'
No matter what.

Joy:
Psalm 94:19: 'When anxiety was great within me, your consolation brought me joy.'
No matter what.

Belonging:
Ephesians 1:5 (NLT): 'God decided in advance to adopt us into his own family by bringing us to himself through Jesus Christ. This is what he wanted to do, and it gave him great pleasure.'
No matter what.

Grace:
2 Corinthians 12:9: 'My grace is sufficient for you.'
No matter what.

Direction:
Jeremiah 29:11 (NLT): '"For I know the plans I have for you," says the LORD. "They are plans for good and not for disaster, to give you a future and a hope."'
No matter what.

Love:
Jeremiah 31:3: 'I have loved [love] you with an everlasting love.'
No matter what.

Father God,

Thank you that when you say 'no matter what', you mean it.
When I say 'But what about . . .' you always interrupt with:
'No matter what.'
And it's true.
Please help me believe it.
Every day.

Amen

Esther's Quest

No matter what

My response:

Day 25

The decree went to everyone, in every language so that absolutely everybody understood. The orders were that on the thirteenth day of the twelfth month, the Jews were allowed to defend themselves against anyone who attacked them. And they were allowed to take any of their victims' belongings they wanted.

Mordecai dictated these orders and they were written in the name of the King. Then they were sealed with Xerxes' signet ring and then delivered all over the area.

Let's look at Acts 2:

Jesus' disciples have had a bit of a roller coaster ride.
They saw Jesus die on the cross.
They saw him alive again.
Then they saw him go into heaven.
And now, they're looking at each other questioningly.
Can you hear what I hear?
They can all hear it.
A sound like wind, blowing down from heaven.
Hang on a minute.
Can you see what I see?

It looks like tongues of fire.

They can all see them.

In fact, before long, the tongues have separated and are resting above each person's head.

Filled with the Holy Spirit, each disciple began to speak about how amazing God is.

And each person listening, whatever their native language, understood what was being said.

Mordecai made sure the decree that went out was understandable to everyone.

It was so important that everyone had to absolutely know what was being said.

God, when he sent the Holy Spirit, made sure that the words spoken about him were accessible to everyone.

No one was to miss out on hearing the wonders of God talked about.

What about us?

When we meet people, socially, at work, in church, and perhaps share our faith,

do we make sure we use language that is accessible?

Understandable?

Jargon-free?

Individual?

It's important.

The decree stated that the Jews must be allowed to
defend themselves against anyone who attacked.
So, the Jews had permission to protect themselves.
But it was their decision.
Up to them whether they accepted the offer.

Our world can be tough, can't it?
But did you know that God gives us permission to
defend ourselves?

Ephesians 6:13–17 (NLT):
*'Put on every piece of God's armor so you will be able
to resist the enemy in the time of evil. Then after the
battle you will still be standing firm. Stand your ground.'*

Put your belt on: Truth.
Protect yourself.
*Psalm 86:11 (NLT): 'Teach me your ways, O LORD, that
I may live according to your truth! Grant me purity of
heart, so that I may honor you.'*

Put your body armour on: God's Righteousness.
Protect your living.
*Colossians 1:10: 'Live a life worthy of the Lord and please
him in every way: bearing fruit in every good work,
growing in the knowledge of God.'*

Put your shoes on: Peace.
Protect your mind.
Philippians 4:7 (NLT): 'Then you will experience God's peace, which exceeds anything we can understand. His peace will guard your hearts and minds as you live in Christ Jesus.'

Hold your shield: Faith.
Protect your believing.
John 6:47 (NLT): 'I tell you the truth, anyone who believes has eternal life.'

Put your helmet on: Salvation.
Protect your knowing.
2 Timothy 1:12: 'I know whom I have believed, and am convinced that he is able to guard what I have entrusted to him until that day.'

Hold your sword: The word of God.
Protect your heart.
Psalm 119:11 (NLT): 'I have hidden your word in my heart, that I might not sin against you.'

Will you accept God's offer?
Put these clothes on each morning and you'll be protected before you've even stepped into the day.

Mordecai may have dictated the orders but they were actually written in the name of the King.

On the King's behalf.

With the King's approval.

As we go through our days, let's remember that whatever we do, we do it in the name of our King.

Or, at least, we should . . .

Colossians 3:17:

'And whatever you do, whether in word or deed, do it all in the name of the Lord Jesus, giving thanks to God the Father through him.'

Father God,

You come to us as individuals.
Help me to follow your example.
To meet people in a way that is accessible for them.
As I go through life, may I consciously clothe and re-clothe myself with your protection.
And do everything in the name of my King.

Amen

Esther's Quest

Be accessible

My response:

Day 26

When Mordecai left the King's presence that day, he was dressed in royal robes and had a crown on his head.

The city of Susa had a big party, the Jews were so happy and celebrating hard! Everywhere that the decree went, it caused Jews to celebrate in style. And even people of other nationalities became Jews!

When Mordecai entered the King's presence, he was dressed as he usually was.
When he left, he was dressed in royal robes.
Being with the King changed Mordecai.

Let's look at John 8:

A man is crouching down, writing on the ground.
With him is a woman.
No one else.
Because everyone who was in the crowd surrounding the man is now walking away from him.
Despite the fact that they are the ones who dragged the woman before him in the first place.
Accusingly.
Selfishly.

With a hidden agenda.
A hidden agenda that backfired on them.
Massively.
The woman had been caught in adultery.
The teachers of the law and the Pharisees had been waiting for a chance to trap Jesus.
To catch him out.
So this opportunity was too good to miss.
They dragged the woman to Jesus:
'The law says we should stone her right now. What do you think, Jesus?'
Without answering, Jesus bent down and started writing on the ground.
'Come on, Jesus. What are you doing? We asked you a question.'
Jesus carried on writing.
They carried on questioning him.
Eventually, he stood.
'OK, go ahead.
Stone her.
But only if you've never done anything wrong yourselves.'
They stared at the ground.
They cast furtive, guilty glances at each other.
They shuffled uneasily.
Shuffling led to turning around.
They knew they'd done things wrong.
One by one, they walked away from Jesus.

What about you?
When you recognize your own weaknesses?

Times you did things wrong?
Fell short?

Do you look away from Jesus?
Afraid to meet his gaze?
Do you turn your back on him and walk away,
just as everyone did that day?
Scared to stand before him?

When God asked Adam, in the Garden of Eden,
'Where are you?'
Adam was afraid.
He knew he'd done wrong.
He'd done the exact thing God told him not to.
And he was scared.
He answered God: 'I heard you in the garden,
and I was afraid . . . so I hid' (Genesis 3:10).
Hid.
Avoided his gaze.
Walked away.
Hid.

Actually, not everyone walked away from Jesus.
One person stood there with him.
The person who'd been dragged there in the first
place.
Whose sin had been acknowledged.
Who didn't leave.
The woman.
As she stood there, not leaving, Jesus spoke to her.

'Where is everyone? Who are the ones who condemn you?'
The woman looks to her right.
She looks to her left.
Then she looks again.
Just to be absolutely sure her eyes aren't deceiving her.
'They've gone. No one's here.'
And then Jesus says something beautiful:
'I don't condemn you, either.'

Those who left did so because they felt condemned.
If they'd stayed, they'd have realized that they didn't need to feel condemned.
Because:

Romans 8:1 (NLT):
'There is no condemnation for those who belong to Christ Jesus.'

What about you?
Does realization of your own sin lead you to walk away from Jesus in shame?
Or do you have the courage to stay with him in your shame . . .
In your hurting.
In your guilt.
In your self-condemnation.
Staying does take courage.

But it's the only way you'll hear him say, 'I don't condemn you.'
The woman learned that despite what she'd done, she could stay.
And she did.

Psalm 103:12 (NLT):
'He has removed our sins as far from us as the east is from the west.'

Mordecai entered the King's presence wearing his usual clothes.
When he left, he wore royal robes and a crown.

The woman entered Jesus' presence in her usual state.
When she left, her life had been changed.
Jesus had forgiven her.
'Go now and leave your life of sin.'

Spending time in Jesus' presence should change us.
After spending time with God, Moses' face lit up.
The fact that he'd been in God's presence changed him, and the change was clear for all to see.
Is it with you?

No one had wanted to join the Jews when they were sad and fearful.

But when people saw the Jews celebrating, they wanted to join in.

Does our delight in our God – at church, at work, day by day – lead others to want to join in?

Acts 2:46,47:
'Every day they (the disciples) continued to meet together . . . praising God . . . And the Lord added to their number daily those who were being saved.'

Father God,

Sometimes, I'm so ashamed of me.
Of things I do, things I say, things I think.
Of attitudes I have towards others.
Condemning attitudes.
I condemn myself sometimes, too.
And the worst of it is, I'm scared to come to you in my shame.
So I walk away.
Carrying my shame with me.
Help me to have courage.
Please.
Courage to stand before you in my shame.
Because only then can you take it from me.
'I don't condemn you.'
Thank you, Father.

Amen

Esther's Quest

I'm not condemned

My response:

Day 27

The partying went on and on! It was brilliant.
Then, when the thirteenth day arrived, the Jews
went ahead and killed their enemies, including the
sons of Haman. But they didn't take any of their
victims' belongings.

After this, Xerxes asked me again if I had any
further requests, so I asked that the Jews in Susa be
allowed to carry on the next day. And the king said
yes, they could carry on with the battle. I also asked
if the ten sons of Haman could be hanged on the
gallows. I know they are already dead but this is
a way of displaying them so that everyone can see
the Jews have triumphed.

The Jews could have taken the belongings from their
victims.
But they didn't.

Let's look at Joshua 7:

The Israelites have just had a wonderful victory.
They've conquered the city of Jericho.

God gave them that victory.
But now God is angry with them.
In fact, in their very next battle, God causes them
to lose.
Spectacularly.
Joshua is devastated and bewildered.
What's going on?
He spends all day face down in prayer before God.

What's going on, Lord?
And God says,
'Come on, Joshua.
Stand up.
Israel has sinned.
They've lied.
They've stolen.
That's why you lost.'

Someone in the Israelite camp was trying to have the
best of both worlds.
They wanted victory in battle, plus things they
shouldn't have.
But that they really, really wanted.
And it was up to Joshua to find out who.

So, the next day, with God's guidance, Joshua
eliminated tribe by tribe.
Clan by clan.
Family by family.

And in the end, he was left with just one man.
Achan.

Joshua asks Achan, 'What have you done?'
This echoes God's words to Eve after she'd eaten the fruit she was told she shouldn't have (see Genesis 3).
What have you done?
Eve tried to make excuses, to remove the blame from herself.
Achan, on the other hand, owns up.
Yes, it was me.

1 Chronicles 29:17 (GOD'S WORD Translation):
'I know, my God, that you examine hearts and delight in honesty.'

How honest are you when God asks, 'What have you done?'
In whatever context.

Maybe over something you shouldn't have done.
'What have you done?'

Or over something you should have done.
'What have you done?'

Maybe over something you have done.
'What have you done?'

Maybe when he asks in an 'I'm interested; tell me
about your day' sort of way:
'What have you done today?'

Or what about when he asks:
'What have you done for me today?'

Matthew 25:40:
*'Whatever you did for one of the least of these brothers
and sisters of mine, you did for me.'*

It turns out that Achan saw beautiful things in Jericho.
Things he shouldn't have had.
But things he took.
He secretly carried them away.
And he buried them under his tent.

He buried them.
He took things he wanted and then he felt so guilty
about it that he kept them hidden.
He couldn't enjoy them at all.
Because he shouldn't have had them.
But they were there, under his tent.
Under the place where he lived.
All the time.
They had no use.
It was as though they were dead.
But they were present.
All the time.

The ten sons of Haman were dead.
And then they were hung on the gallows.
Wait: How can that be?
People are hung up on gallows to die, not the other way round.
Perhaps Esther didn't want to leave dead things lying around.
She wanted them out of the way.

What about us?
Do we get rid of things that are – or should be – dead to us?

Romans 6:11 (NLT):
'So you also should consider yourselves to be dead to the power of sin and alive to God through Christ Jesus.'

Don't leave 'the power of sin' lying around.
Don't keep it buried within your day-to-day life.

Hanging up the corpses was proof of victory.
As you metaphorically hang up the corpses of things that are now dead to you, remember that they are proof of victory.
Those things no longer have power over you.

1 Corinthians 15:54:
'Death has been swallowed up in victory.'

God said to Joshua, 'The reason things aren't working out is that Israel is deliberately disobeying me.'

Israel is disobeying.
Even though it was only one member of the Israelite nation, Achan, who disobeyed, all were affected.

In the same way, when one member of the church is hurting, the whole church hurts.

1 Corinthians 12:26:
'If one part suffers, every part suffers with it; if one part is honoured, every part rejoices with it.'

When Esther's people hurt, she hurt.
And when her people rejoiced, she rejoiced.

We should do the same.

Father God,

Sometimes, I am tempted to hold on to things.
Unhelpful things.
Help me to get rid of them rather than keep them
buried within me.
And Father, help me to love your church.
Your people.
To recognize when they are hurting.
To hurt with them.
And to dare to be vulnerable enough to let people
hurt with me.
So we can truly be the body of Christ, with you at
the head.

Amen

Esther's Quest

What have I done?

My response:

Day 28

On the fourteenth and fifteenth days, the Jews rested from fighting and celebrated instead. We Jews certainly know how to throw a good party!

This celebration, we called it the feast of Purim, would became an annual tradition. We wanted to regularly celebrate and remember God's faithfulness. Mordecai and I wrote to all the Jews to confirm that Purim was an established feast from now on and just to assure them that all is now well.

The Jews took a break from fighting.
Enough was enough.
It was time to stop the struggle for a while.
The busy-ness.
The being on the go all the time.

Does that sound familiar?
Maybe not taking a break.
But struggling and being so busy you never stop?
God says to you,

'I am your shepherd!
You have everything you need.

I have settled you down in lush meadows,
I find you quiet pools to drink from.
True to my word,
I let you pause . . .'
(Psalm 23:1–3 based on *The Message*).

Purim is still celebrated today.
The entire book of Esther is read aloud in the
synagogue.
So everyone can hear and be reminded of God's
goodness.
Of his sovereignty.
Of the way he worked in the life of a girl who became
Queen and saved her people.
Every year, daily life pauses as Jews remember God's
goodness to them.
His faithfulness.
His love.
His mercy.
His grace.
His care.
His guidance.
His protection.
His encouragement.
His leading.

'Remember God's goodness' is written into their
calendar.

How's your diary looking?
Time to struggle: check.
Time to be over-busy: check.
Time to fight things: check.
Time to worry: check.
Time to dash around: check.
Time to remember God's goodness: check?

It can be hard to stop.
To pause.
To breathe.
To take time to simply be with God just because.
To remember his goodness.

Thankfully, in that goodness, God gave us a way to do it.
A way to pause.
A way to take time out.
A way to focus on him.

Exodus 20:8–11 (NLT):

*'Remember to observe the Sabbath day
by keeping it holy.
You have six days each week for your ordinary work, but
the seventh day is a Sabbath day of rest dedicated to the
LORD your God . . .
For in six days the LORD made the heavens, the earth,
the sea, and everything in them;
but on the seventh day he rested.
That is why the LORD blessed the Sabbath day
and set it apart as holy.'*

He gave us Sabbath.
Sabbath rest.
Maybe, for you, Sabbath is a Sunday.
Or maybe it's not.
Either way, remember to observe a Sabbath time in
your week.

Let's look at a couple of things in the Exodus passage.

'Remember to observe the Sabbath day.'
Remember.
Make a note of it.
Write it into your diary.
In ink.
Today is special.
And remember to keep it that way.
It's God's day.
God's and yours.

Remember God's goodness.

And what does God, in his goodness, suggest you do
on Sabbath days?
Well, follow his seventh-day example:
Rest.

Take a break from the daily grind of life.
Spend time not working.
Not being busy.

Not exhausting yourself.
On days one to six of creation, God had been busy
making the world (Genesis 1).
On day seven, he rested.

Remember God's goodness.

God 'blessed the Sabbath day' – rest – and set it apart
as holy.

Day seven is the only day God blessed.
He looked at days one to six.
And he saw that they were 'good'.
But he blessed day seven.
He blessed the day
on
which
he
rested.

One meaning of the word 'blessed' is 'extol'.
Extol means 'to praise highly'.

So, God highly praises the taking of rest.
He gives rest to us.

Joshua 1:13 (NLT):
'The LORD your God is giving you . . . rest.'

Is giving you.
Not has.
Or will.
Is.

You can take a moment to pause,
to reflect,
to rest,
to remember God's goodness . . .
Any.
Time.
You.
Want.

Psalm 34:8:
'Taste and see that the LORD is good; blessed is the one who takes refuge in him.'

Purim today is firmly embedded in the Jewish calendar.
But the very first time it was held, when Esther was Queen, it was a spontaneous outburst of celebration.

When was the last time your heart burst into spontaneous celebration of God?
When love for him just bubbled up inside you?

Psalm 103:1 (NLT):
*'Let all that I am praise the LORD; with my whole heart,
I will praise his holy name.'*

Remember to remember God's goodness.

Father God,

I have something to celebrate.
All the time.
Because you are with me.
All the time.
Thank you that you created rest.
More than created it; you blessed it.
I know I do too much.
I know I find it hard to stop.
But even you rested.
You set me an example of rest.
That's how important rest is.
I know.
But I find it hard.
Help me to follow your example.
To make the most of it.
To look for it.
To schedule 'you' times into my diary.
But to be taken by surprise by them, too.

Amen

Esther's Quest

Remember God's
goodness

My response:

Day 29

Mordecai has been promoted. He is now second in rank to King Xerxes!

Well, if anyone deserves it, he does. Almost everyone likes and respects him, especially the Jews. It is because he has always wanted the best for people and has defended and spoken up on behalf of the Jews.

Mordecai has been rewarded.
For his consistency.
For doing the right thing.
He wasn't looking to be rewarded.
Perhaps didn't even know there was a possibility of reward.
All he wanted to do was live every day honourably.
Obediently.
Faithfully.

Let's look at Abram, Genesis 12:

'Leave your country.
Leave your family home.'

Day 29

That's what God said to Abram.
The first (recorded) thing God ever said to Abram.

'OK, I'll set off for . . .'

*'You don't need to know that yet.
I know where you're going.'*

'Well, that's great, but . . .'

'I will show you where you're going.'

So, God is saying,
leave the places you know,
the people you know,
the life you know,
and go somewhere you don't know.
Because I know.

Would that be enough for Abram?
To trust his not knowing to an all-knowing God?
Would it be enough for you?
Is it enough for you?

God goes on to say, 'I will bless you, Abram.'
I will bless you.
I will.
I won't tell you where you're going.
But I will tell you that where you're going is blessed.

God's blessings are not dependent on us knowing what lies ahead of us.

They're not dependent on us knowing the plan.

Jeremiah 29:11 (NLT):

'"For I know the plans I have for you," says the LORD. "They are plans for good and not for disaster, to give you a future and a hope."'

How trustworthy was Abram's God?
100 per cent.

How trustworthy is your God?
100 per cent.

Proverbs 3:5,6 (NLT):

'Trust in the LORD with all your heart; do not depend on your own understanding. Seek his will in all you do, and he will show you which path to take.'

So, how trusting are you of your 100 per cent trustworthy God?
100 per cent?
70 per cent?
50 per cent?
20 per cent?
Those times when he says to you:
'I won't tell you where you're going.
But I promise there'll be blessing along the way.
Trust me.'

And sometimes, not knowing your future is actually a
blessing in itself.
God knows what will happen in life.
The ups and downs.
Highs and lows.
Laughter and tears that will come your way.
Your future is in his hands.
He knows.
So that you don't have to know just yet.
God gives you light for the present.
And assurance that,
when your future emerges from the shadows
to be lit up as your present,
there will be blessing in the midst.

How trusting was Abram of his 100 per cent
trustworthy God?

Genesis 12:4 (ISV):
'So Abram left.'

He left.
He stepped out of the life he knew.
And he stepped into the knowing of God.

Mordecai did the right thing without thinking about
whether he'd see reward.
Abram stepped out in faith without knowing where
he was going.

Both men brought – and bring – glory to God by the way in which they lived their lives.
By their consistency.
By their faith.
By their trust.

You can, too, you know.

1 Peter 2:12 (NLT):
'They will see your honorable behavior, and they will give honor (glory) to God.'

Abram knew the one who knew.
And that was enough.

Father God,

So often, I look at my life,
look at where I'm going,
and I don't know.
I just don't know.
And then I worry that I don't know.
But you know.
May knowing the one who knows
always be enough for me.
Help me to trust you.
To follow you.
And receive your blessings along the way.

Amen

Esther's Quest

Step into the
knowing of God

My response:

Day 30

I've just read through my diary. Wow, so much has happened in ten years. When I started this diary, I was just Esther. Now I am Queen Esther. Change in name, change in home, change in clothes.

Sometimes I lose sight of myself a bit – it's easy to do with all the busyness of royal life. But Mordecai is there to remind me, just as he always has done.

Reminding me that I am still the same me inside. Reminding me that I am privileged. And that with privilege comes responsibility.

Esther's life was busy.
Busy with good things.
But still busy.
Maybe your life is busy.
Busy with good things.
But still busy.

Jesus' disciples had days like that.
Days when they were busy with good things.
Helping people.

Serving God.
But some of these days were days when they were
also too busy to even stop for a bite to eat.
They were on the go.
All the time.
Let's look at Mark 6:

The disciples had been away.
They'd been travelling around,
talking to people,
preaching to people,
driving demons out of people,
praying for people . . .
And then they came back.
Full of all they'd seen and done, the first thing they
did was find Jesus.
They wanted to tell him all about it.
To share their experiences with him.
To spend time with him.
But, what happens?
They struggle to get a word in.
It's mayhem.
People coming.
People going.
People weaving in and out.
No time for anything other than keeping their heads
above the commotion.
No time even to eat.
A cacophony of sounds and voices blur into noise.

And then a voice speaks clearly into the chaos.
'Come on. Come with me . . .'
It's Jesus.

Mark 6:31:
*'Then, because so many people were coming and going
that they did not even have a chance to eat, he said to
them, "Come with me by yourselves to a quiet place and
get some rest."'*

Come with me.
*I can see you're exhausted. So stop thinking, and talking,
and doing . . . and just come.*
By yourselves.
*Come alone. Yes, there are lots of people. But you're one
of them. And you matter.*
To a quiet place.
*Where you are right now is anything but quiet. And
that's OK. But sometimes you need a change of scene. Of
pace. Of being. A quiet place where you and I can be 'just
us' for a while.*
And get some rest.
Take a break.
Give yourself permission to rest.
*And if I'm telling you to do so – which I am – it must
be OK.*

Esther's life had changed almost beyond recognition.
The girl who became Queen.
But something didn't change.

The presence of Mordecai.
He was always there for Esther, no matter what.

Just as God is always there.
No matter what.

Mordecai reminded Esther that she was still the same
person inside.
And it's what's inside that counts.

1 Samuel 16:7:
*'The LORD does not look at the things people look at.
People look at the outward appearance,
but the LORD looks at the heart.'*

God looks at hearts.
What does he see when he looks at yours?

Mordecai also reminded Esther that her position of
great privilege didn't mean she could back out of
responsibility.
If anything, the responsibility to do the right thing
was even greater.

1 John 3:1:
*'See what great love the Father has lavished on us, that
we should be called children of God! And that is what
we are!'*

We have a privilege greater than any other: to live and
serve as children of God.
The disciples had the same privilege.
And Jesus showed them that alongside,
they had a responsibility to rest.
To pause.
To take time out so that they were able to take time
in amongst the crowd.
In amongst the demands and busyness of life.
And we need to do the same.

Both Esther and the disciples needed responsibility
reminders.
And Mordecai and Jesus did just that.

Responsibility reminders are good.

Doing the right thing is good.
It honours God.
It's a privilege.
Even when it's hard.
When it's scary.
When it's inconvenient.
When it's confusing.

And Jesus' voice echoes.
On and on.
Into the chaos of life.
On and on.

Day 30

Directly to you:

'Come with me . . . and get some rest.'

'Come with me.'

Wherever I am.
Whatever I do.
When you're busy.
And when you're not.
I want to share life with you:

'Come with me.'

205

Father God,

Thank you for Esther.
For her life.
For her example.
For her humility.
I'm glad she had Mordecai.
And I'm glad I have you.
Speaking into my chaos.
Guiding me.
Helping me.
Reminding me of who I am:
Your child.
I'm so blessed.
Help me to keep following you.
And sharing with you.
Every day.

Amen

Esther's Quest

Come with me

My response:

Notes

DAY 4

[1] http://www.answers.com/Q/How_many_Israelites_came_out_of_the_Wilderness_with_Moses (accessed 6.12.16).

DAY 17

[1] http://biblehub.com/topical/e/elkanah.htm (accessed 1.12.16).

30 Days with David

*A devotional journey with
the shepherd boy*

Emily Owen

By imagining the diaries of familiar figures from the Bible, Emily Owen draws us into their lives. She then leads us in contemplation, often taking a surprising direction. Gently challenging, each day draws us closer to God.

In *30 Days with David* we follow David from his anointment as king, through to Goliath's challenge and finally to his marriage to Michal. Along the way we are encouraged to keep our eyes on God, to know God is with us and to chase God's heart – just like David.

978-1-78078-449-6

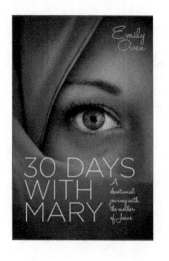

30 Days with Mary

*A devotional journey with
the mother of Jesus*

Emily Owen

What must it have been like to be Mary, the mother of the Son of God?

In *30 Days with Mary* we look at her diary, sharing in her trials and challenges, fears and joys, from her teenage encounter with an angel, to the awesomeness of realizing her crucified son is alive again. The diary excerpts lead us in contemplation, challenging our own relationship with Christ and, in so doing, draw us closer to him.

978-1-86024-935-8

Authentic

We trust you enjoyed reading this book from Authentic. If you want to be informed of any new titles from this author and other releases you can sign up to the Authentic newsletter by contacting us:

By post:
Authentic Media Limited
PO Box 6326
Bletchley
Milton Keynes
MK1 9GG

E-mail:
info@authenticmedia.co.uk

Follow us: